"Hear, my son, your father's instruction...." (Proverbs 1:8)

The book of Proverbs contains a series of short sentences expressing God's wisdom. It's written by a dad who loves his sons and daughters, who wants the best for them, and who is crying out for them to follow God and His Word—not their own interests, desires, and passions.

Though Proverbs lacks the stories found in the Gospels and other Old Testament books, it contains the wisdom of God in just a few words. God knew that His people would need to be reminded again and again regarding how they were to think, speak, and act. So He inspired Proverbs to do just that.

Contrary to the world's call to "live and learn," the promise of Proverbs is "learn and live." Studying and following these proverbs will make you a wise and righteous person with a rich, full life.

Approach Proverbs as a learner, a teachable person who desires to soak up its lessons. If you do, you'll gain what Proverbs offers: the opportunity to understand God's wise sayings; to develop discernment; to receive instruction on how to live righteously, justly, and fairly; to choose a life direction and purpose; to obey God's wisdom from the heart; and to never stop learning from the Word of God.

Papa Mike has studied the endless fountain of truth that is the book of Proverbs ever since he became a Christian forty-eight years ago—and he is still learning from it today. Over the ten years Papa Mike has spent writing this study, he has fallen deeply in love with this book and its wisdom. His prayer is that you would as well.

Papa Mike's Bible Study on Proverbs comes from a father's heart that beams with love for his children and their children. The study opens with an overview of Proverbs, then leads the reader through twenty-five character building principles. It contains Papa Mike's comments on select passages, stories from his life, and his prayers for you. You'll also work through assignments designed by Papa Mike to help you apply this book's marvelous truths. If you long to be truly wise, *Papa Mike's Bible Study on Proverbs* is a trustworthy guide to the most profound compilation of wisdom you could ever ponder.

"When I was a son to my father, tender and the only son in the sight of my mother, then he taught me and said to me, 'Let your heart hold fast my words; keep my commandments and live.'" (Proverbs 4:3–4)

PAPA MIKE'S BIBLE STUDY ON
PROVERBS

PAPA MIKE'S BIBLE STUDY on PROVERBS
(As Well as My Personal Thoughts and Life Stories)

Copyright © 2023 Mike Hefner

ISBN: 978-1-956220-57-5

All rights reserved. No portion of this book may be reproduced mechanically, electronically, or by any other means, including photocopying, without the written permission of the author. It is illegal to copy the book, post it to a website, or distribute it by any other means without permission from the author.

Unless otherwise noted, all Scripture references in this book are taken from the New American Standard Bible®, Copyright © 1960, 1971, 1977, 1995 by The Lockman Foundation. All rights reserved.

The "NASB," "NAS," "New American Standard Bible," and "New American Standard," are trademarks registered in the United States Patent and Trademark Office by The Lockman Foundation. Use of these trademarks requires the permission of The Lockman Foundation.

Select Scripture quotations are from The ESV® Bible (The Holy Bible, English Standard Version®), copyright © 2001 by Crossway, a publishing ministry of Good News Publishers. Used by permission. All rights reserved.

Select Scripture quotations from The Authorized (King James) Version. Rights in the Authorized Version in the United Kingdom are vested in the Crown. Reproduced by permission of the Crown's patentee, Cambridge University Press.

Expert Press
2 Shepard Hills Court
Little Rock, AR 72223
www.ExpertPress.net

Editing by Lori Price
Proofreading by Heather Dubnick
Text design and composition by Emily Fritz
Cover design by Casey Fritz

PAPA MIKE'S
BIBLE STUDY ON
PROVERBS
(AS WELL AS MY PERSONAL THOUGHTS AND LIFE STORIES)

MIKE HEFNER

I dedicate this book to Diane Hefner for the forty-six years that she has been my beloved wife. I agree with Proverbs that her worth is above jewels, and she is a wonderful gift from God.

I have never, not once, had any concern about whether I should trust Diane. She is totally trustworthy!

Diane has been God's gift in helping me become all God wanted me to be. She helped me manage people in my corporate jobs, as a missionary with FamilyLife, and while on staff at Bible Church of Little Rock. She shared her wisdom with me in how to deal with difficult situations. She and I would also discuss the content of my Sunday school lessons, how I would proceed in a counseling session, and finally, in developing the next steps in parenting our children. In all these things, she always prayed for me. That was a real confidence builder in this man. She also proofed many of my work documents, Sunday School lessons, and Bible studies for grammar, spelling, and content. She was, and continues to be, invaluable to me!

Her children and grandchildren have richly blessed her,
and she truly does fear the Lord.

I am one blessed man!

CONTENTS

Foreword		1
PART I. OVERVIEW OF PROVERBS		**3**
Introduction	A Letter to My Children's Children and Their Children	5
	My Testimony	7
	Getting to Know the God of Salvation	13
Chapter 1	Information Concerning This Wonderful Book	23
Chapter 2	What David and Solomon Told Their Sons about Living	33
Chapter 3	The Overriding Message of Proverbs	41
Chapter 4	The Five Purposes of the Book of Proverbs	43
Chapter 5	Wisdom Is Shouting	49
Chapter 6	Walk in the Light of His Word and Wisdom	51
Chapter 7	Human Responsibility and Divine Response	55
PART II. TWENTY-FIVE CHARACTER BUILDING PRINCIPLES		**63**
Chapter 8	Principle #1 – The Fear of the Lord	65
Chapter 9	Principle # 2 – Love Wisdom and Righteousness / Reject Foolishness and Wickedness	71
Chapter 10	Principle #3 – Receive Counsel	81
Chapter 11	Principle #4 – Guard Your Heart	87
Chapter 12	Principle #5 – Be Open to Reproofs and Rebukes	105
Chapter 13	Principle #6 – Be Careful How and Where You Walk as Well as Whom You Walk With	111
Chapter 14	Principle #7 – Accept God's Discipline and Be Obedient	115
Chapter 15	Principle # 8 – How to Deal with Temptation	119

Chapter 16	Principle #9 – How to Handle Money	123
Chapter 17	Principle #10 – The Value of Hard Work	135
Chapter 18	Principle # 11 – Control Your Anger	145
Chapter 19	Principle #12 – Be a Good Listener and a God Honoring Speaker	149
Chapter 20	Principle #13 – The Right View of Sex	157
Chapter 21	Principle #14 – Daughters, Be an Excellent Wife	159
Chapter 22	Principle # 15 – Embrace Humility and Reject Pride	163
Chapter 23	Principle # 16 – The Value of a Good Name and Integrity	165
Chapter 24	Principle #17 – Be Honest and Avoid Lying at All Costs	169
Chapter 25	Principle #18 – Be a Good Friend	173
Chapter 26	Principle #19 – Trust God	179
Chapter 27	Principle # 20 – Be Good Parents	183
Chapter 28	Principle #21 – What Causes and Eliminates Strife	187
Chapter 29	Principle #22 – Be a Good Neighbor	193
Chapter 30	Three Last Principles	
	Principle #23 – Be a Blessing to Your Parents	195
	Principle #24 – Be Joyful and Cheerful	196
	Principle #25 – Leave an Inheritance	196

PART 3. CONCLUSION 197

Legacy 199
Memorial Stones 203
Books That Have Impacted My Life 209

FOREWORD

> "Follow my example as I follow the example of Christ."

These are the instructions of the Apostle Paul to the Corinthians (1 Corinthians 11:1 - NIV). These are also the instructions Mike Hefner could have used as he discipled me and many others.

Mike is a passionate follower of Jesus Christ and a student of the Bible. His dedication to learning, growing, and teaching God's Word is unlike any that I've seen. He's by no means perfect, but he strives to be like Jesus in every area of his life.

Mike came into my life when we joined the ministry of FamilyLife. From there, God began to knit our lives together in many ways. Mike has been my Sunday School teacher, Care Group leader, elder, mentor, confidant, counselor, and friend.

His untiring work ethic is an example to me to this day. The way he loves his wife challenges me to up my game continually. And his ever-ready servant nature inspires me to do more for others and the Kingdom.

It's hard to estimate the impact Mike has had on my life. A few of his phrases are forever emblazoned on my mind (and tongue). Among these are "it's okay", "live before an audience of One", and the one I live with daily: "Priority Drives Behavior!"

The word "disciple" means learner. This exemplifies Mike Hefner. And he is also a disciple maker following the command of Jesus in Matthew 28:19-20.

Mike has poured his life into dozens and has consistently pointed them to God's Word as THE Source for wisdom, counsel, and truth.

In this study of Proverbs, Mike once again shares his keen insights. As you read his thoughts, you can sense his shepherd's heart as he pleads with you to heed the counsel of this amazing book.

Proverbs is one of the most practical books in the Bible. And Mike is one of the most practical people I know. This is a powerful combination that has produced a very practical resource for knowing how we are to live.

The way Mike uses God's Word reminds me of how the Psalmist described God's Word in Psalm 119:105:

> "Your Word is a lamp to my feet and a light to my path."

As you read this study I'm confident that Mike would encourage you to open your mind and heart to deeply ponder the life changing Truth that is contained in the book of Proverbs.

I praise God for Mike Hefner and am blessed to call him my friend. My life is richer because of how he has poured into me. He has poured hours of his life into creating this study. As you read this, I'm convinced that your life will be blessed by him also.

Thank you, Mike, for your labor of love in putting this together. If you could hear Jesus now, I'm sure he would be saying, "Well done, my good and faithful servant."

For the glory of Christ,

MICHAEL DELON
June 2023

PART I.
OVERVIEW OF PROVERBS

INTRODUCTION

A Letter to My Children's Children and Their Children

Dear Kids,

Some of you might be wondering why a relative would write a Bible study with his personal thoughts on Proverbs as well as his life stories. A long time ago, the Lord laid on my heart to be like Abel, "Though he is dead, he still speaks" (Hebrews 11:4). Therefore, knowing that one day I will pass on from this life to the next, this is the only way that I can still speak after my death.

This Bible study is also a memorial to what God has done in and through Dee Dee and Papa Mike.

I have written this Bible study with the following things in mind:

First, I desire for each of you to come to know the Lord Jesus Christ and to make Him Lord of your life. This is my way of showing you how that can be accomplished.

Second, I want you to see the call on your life to tell others about Jesus Christ. Dee Dee's and my desire was to teach God's Word to our children and challenge them to teach His Word to their children, and so on and so on.

> Listen, O my people, to my instruction; incline your ears to the words of my mouth. I will open my mouth in a parable; I will utter dark sayings of old, which we have heard and known, and our fathers have told us. We will not conceal them from their children, but tell to the generation to come the praises of the Lord, and His strength and His wondrous works that He has done. For He established a testimony in Jacob and appointed a law in Israel, which He commanded our fathers that they should teach them to their children, that the generation to come might know, even the children yet to be born that they may arise and tell them to their children, that they should [1] put their confidence in God [2] and not forget the works of God, [3] but keep His commandments. [4] And not be like their fathers, a stubborn and rebellious generation, a generation that did not prepare its heart and whose spirit was not faithful to God. (Psalm 78:1–8) [Brackets are the author's.]

Third, to help you see the marvelous truths of this book, I have included assignments that I hope you will complete. These sections will be highlighted by the words,

> "Papa Mike's Assignments."

Fourth, it will contain my personal commentary on this wonderful book. These thoughts will be at the 5,000-foot level and not on each individual verse. My thoughts will be preceded by,

> "Papa Mike's Comments."

Fifth, it will contain stories from my life, which will be highlighted by the words,

> "Papa Mike's Life."

Sixth, it will contain my prayers for you, which will be preceded by the words,

> "Papa Mike's Prayer."

Love,
Papa Mike

MY TESTIMONY

I was raised in a very caring, religious, and moral home in Little Rock, Arkansas, in a neighborhood called "The Heights." From my perspective, our family did not emphasize the importance of having a relationship with Christ. But I do praise God for my parents for the many excellent character qualities they instilled in me. My upbringing gave me a background in the Bible, which God would use to keep me as moral as a young man can be without knowing Christ.

After I had graduated from the University of Arkansas (U of A) with a degree in industrial management in December 1973, I started working in Little Rock, Arkansas, at Teletype Corporation. It was during the next ten months that God worked in my life to cause me to question the values I had embraced and my life goals. He did that by showing me how everything I thought was important was built on shifting sand.

The first blow to my values was in wanting to be like my mom and dad by finding a wife and starting a family. When I was getting my industrial management degree, I became friends with a married couple. They would invite me to dinner often. It was a wonderful time, and it made me long for a wife. From what I could tell, they had a perfect marriage. After I moved to Little Rock, I heard they had moved to Little Rock also. I called them to see if we could get together. They asked if I would come to dinner. When I arrived, they told me they had something to tell me. They informed me they were getting a divorce but that it was okay. It was not a big deal to them, but I was devastated. I honestly think I was more devastated than they were. I had also met several people at work who were divorced. My dream of finding a wife, having a family, and living together for a lifetime was crumbling right before my eyes.

The second blow to my values was my belief that I was equipped for making a good living. One day at Teletype, I noticed my coworker left his pay stub in plain sight. Since we sat right next to each other, it was hard for me not to notice that his salary was 50 percent higher than mine, and we were doing the same work. Later that day, I went to see my boss. I told him I should not have seen my coworker's pay stub, but I did. I was respectful, but I asked him if there was a reason that I made significantly less than my coworker. He told me my coworker was an engineer and if I wanted to make that much, all I had to do was get an engineering degree. The very next day, I called the dean of industrial engineering at the U of A and told him I wanted to get an engineering degree. He asked me what my undergraduate degree was, and I told him industrial management. He told me an industrial engineer would be the way to go. I said that would be great. He told me he would get back with me in a few days because he had to review what classes I had taken while getting my industrial management degree. He called me back later that week and told me I could get a degree in industrial engineering in two semesters by taking eighteen hours of upper-level engineering courses each semester. I told him to sign me up. He then informed me there was a problem. Three of the classes I needed to take were not offered the next year, but he told me he would find three professors to take me through those courses so I could get credit and graduate. WOW! Is that not a God thing? The rest is history. I did go to U of A in the fall of 1974 and graduated in the spring of 1975 with a degree in industrial engineering.

The third blow to my values was in my "purpose in life." In the spring of 1974, I started thinking about my life, and it seemed the more I thought about it, the more my direction and purpose became increasingly empty and self-serving. It seemed that I really did not have a "good" purpose for living.

Just as God paved the way for me to get an engineering degree, He also provided a place for me to live at the university. I contacted a couple of friends, told them I was coming back to the U of A, and asked if they could help me find a place to live. They put me in touch with a friend who lived right across from the engineering building. Now, for the good news—the owner of the apartments was charging fifty dollars a month, including water! That was unheard of at the university. I called the landlady and found out someone was moving out in the summer. A few more calls, and the apartment was mine. Another God thing!

Now, let's fast forward to my first day of classes. I walked into my Operations Research class, and there was a pretty sophomore. So, after class I politely introduced myself. I asked her out, but she would not go out with me. Later, I asked her over to study for our first quiz. We talked some about the quiz, but her focus was on Christ and His Word, which was fine with me since I was religious. During our conversation, I told her that the Bible was a bunch of stories—some true and some not. Her response stopped me in my tracks. She told me that I must be God. She explained if I was going to be the judge of which stories were true and which were not true, then I must be God. I had no answer for her, but it really made me think.

Then, I found out her sorority needed someone to clean up after meals, and the pay was great: "You could eat whatever they did not eat." At that time, I was living on a shoestring budget. Once I started working at Diane's sorority, I met a lot of her Christian friends. I discovered that several of them were attending University Baptist Church. I told them I would be glad to take them to church. It would give me another opportunity to spend some time with Diane since she really had no interest in me at all except to share Christ and what He had done in her life! The next Sunday, I picked up Diane and a few of her friends, and I walked into a Baptist church for the first time in my life! And as I recall, I knew at once these people were different. They really enjoyed being there. The people loved to sing, and the preacher, H.D. McCarty, loved what he was teaching. He taught from the Bible—verse by verse. Well, to make a long story short, in less than five weeks I found myself getting out of bed around midnight and telling God that I was a sinner, I wanted to place all my sin on Christ, and I wanted Him to take total control of my life! I then went back to sleep, but oh, what a difference Christ made! I woke up a new creature in Christ, old things had passed away and new things had come (2 Corinthians 5:17)! Was I ever different! As Diane would tell you, I was radically saved. I had a love for God, His Word, and His people; I did not want to do the things I was doing just the week before. Praise the Lord. He set me on a new course—a course filled with love, life, and, most importantly, purpose!

During my spring semester, Diane went to work for Ethyl Corporation in Baton Rouge, Louisiana. Our relationship became one of letters and phone calls. In May of 1975, I graduated and went to work for Union Carbide south of Houston, Texas. More letters and phone calls. Once again, God's sovereign hand was working. During that time apart, I continued to grow in the Lord, which allowed our relationship to change from one in which I came to Diane for spiritual advice to one where she looked to me for advice.

By the summer of 1976, I had purchased a three-bedroom home. I remember walking out the back door of my new home and asking God whether I would ever get married. My desire was to have a wife and raise a family. Whenever I prayed about Diane's and my relationship, it seemed that what He wanted me to do was enjoy her as a friend. But during the fall when I prayed about our relationship, God was somewhat quiet. I saw Diane over Thanksgiving at my parents' home in Little Rock. While there I told her I was going to continue to pray about our relationship. Her comment was that "she would pray for me." I went to see Diane again over Christmas, and I was still unclear as to God's will for us. But I had decided as soon as I got back to Houston, I would fast and pray about what the future would hold. Again, her comment was that "she would pray for me." Four days later, I was confident that I needed to ask Diane to marry me. I called her, and she asked if I wanted to come to ask her father for his permission. The next day I walked into my boss's office and told him I needed a couple of days off. I had already used up all my vacation for that year. He asked me why. I told him I needed to fly to Fayetteville to ask Diane's dad if I could marry her. Needless to say, it took him by surprise since everyone knew that I did not have a girlfriend; he had never heard me talking about a "Diane." My boss gave me permission. I flew to Fayetteville, where I obtained permission from Diane's dad to marry her; six months later, we were married at University Baptist Church in Fayetteville.

As Paul Harvey would say, "And now you know the rest of the story."

Here is a quick summary of how God used us from the time we got married until today.

We lived in Houston (League City) for two years. These were growth years for both Diane and me. We had a wonderful church and pastor. It was when we lived in League City that Aaron was born.

God then took us to Los Angeles, California, in 1979. What a culture shock to this Arkansas boy! We joined Grace Brethren Church of Long Beach, where David Hocking was the pastor. Soon after joining a Sunday School class, they asked us to join their discipleship ministry. God used us in the lives of the people we discipled. I challenged men to have a daily quiet time with God and to make their relationship with their wives and family a higher priority. What a joy it was to see God work in these men. The best thing about living in Los Angeles was the church and the ministry of David Hocking. He taught us so much.

In 1981, God moved us to Charleston, West Virginia. It wasn't exactly where we wanted to be, but God had other plans. While in Charleston, we joined the Bible Center Church, and in 1983, I became an adult Sunday school teacher. This is where God began to truly burden my heart for families. Once again, God used us in many people's lives to make them examine their commitment to Christ and their walk with the Lord. We still look back on those years in Charleston as some very precious times. Marcie and Ben were born there, and Marcie underwent open heart surgery at the age of nineteen months. While we were in Charleston, God worked in our lives to bring us to the decision to homeschool our children starting in the fall of 1993 when Aaron was in the ninth grade, Marcie in seventh, and Ben in fourth.

The very next year, God moved us to Houston, Texas, where He led us to join a small independent Baptist church in Katy. Once again, I became the adult Sunday school teacher and a deacon. Diane and I were blessed to watch our church grow from sixty to over 250 people. While there, we met some wonderful people, who became our best friends (the Greenlaws, Tapps, Mixons, Alexanders, and Spenas).

In 2001, God started moving in our lives to leave secular work and go into full-time Christian service. In time, we joined FamilyLife and became Campus Crusade for Christ (CRU) missionaries. FamilyLife was located in Little Rock. In November 2002, this boy came home to Little Rock after being gone for twenty-seven years. I served as the Director of Purchasing/Materials Manager and Diane worked in the content department.

In 2002, we joined Bible Church of Little Rock and in 2006, I became an elder. In 2007, I left FamilyLife to become the church administrator at Bible Church. I was in that position until 2017. From 2009 until the beginning of 2019, I was the chairman of the elders.

Late in 2019, we left the Bible Church and joined Summit Church of Saline County. At Summit Church, I became the director of the men's ministry.

In the summer of 2021, we moved to Xenia, Ohio, to be closer to Marcie and Ben and their families. We joined Dayton Avenue Baptist Church. One year later, they made me the head of their men's ministry. The move to Ohio has been wonderful.

God is so good!

GETTING TO KNOW THE GOD OF SALVATION

It starts with the gospel, which is "the good news of salvation."

> "For I am not ashamed of the gospel, for it is the power of God for salvation to everyone who believes, to the Jew first and also to the Greek" (Romans 1:16).

God is merciful and loving, and He draws us to Himself with lovingkindness.

> "God is love" (1 John 4:8).

> "The Lord appeared to him from afar, saying, 'I have loved you with an everlasting love; Therefore, I have drawn you with lovingkindness'" (Jeremiah 31:3).

He is also a perfect judge, whose standard is perfection—which means "no sinning."

> "Therefore you are to be perfect, as your heavenly Father is perfect" (Matthew 5:48).

Sin is transgressing or going against God's law and includes such things as lying, lust, cheating, deceit, evil thoughts, immoral behavior, and more—the list is endless. All of us do evil, and there is nothing in us that is good.

> "As it is written, 'There is none righteous, not even one; there is none who understands, there is none who seeks for God; all have turned aside, together they have become useless; there is none who does good, there is not even one'" (Romans 3:10-12).

> "For all have sinned and fall short of the glory of God" (Romans 3:23).

> We were dead in our trespasses and sin (Ephesians 2:12).

What happens at the end of this life without Christ:

> "For the wages of sin is death" (Romans 6:23).

> "The soul who sins will die" (Ezekiel 18:4).

> "Who keeps lovingkindness for thousands, who forgives iniquity, transgression and sin; yet He will by no means leave the guilty unpunished" (Exodus 34:7).

> "Then I saw a great white throne and Him who sat upon it, from whose presence earth and heaven fled away, and no place was found for them. And I saw the dead, the great and the small, standing before the throne, and books were opened; and another book was opened, which is the book of life *with the names of the people who have accepted Jesus as their Lord and Savior*, and the dead were judged from the things which were written in the books, according to their deeds. And the sea gave up the dead which were in it, and death and Hades gave up the dead which were in them; and they were judged, every one of them according to their deeds. Then death and Hades were thrown into the lake of fire. This is the second death, the lake of fire. And if anyone's name was not found written in the book of life, he was thrown into the lake of fire" (Revelation 20:11-15). [Italicized portion is the author's.]

> "But for the cowardly and unbelieving and abominable and murderers and immoral persons and sorcerers and idolaters and all liars, their part will be in the lake that burns with fire and brimstone, which is the second death" (Revelation 21:8).

We are storing up the wrath of God.

> "He who believes in the Son has eternal life; but he who does not obey the Son will not see life, but the wrath of God abides on him" (John 3:36).

> "For the wrath of God is revealed from heaven against all ungodliness and unrighteousness of men who suppress the truth in unrighteousness, because that which is known about God is evident within them; for God made it evident to them" (Romans 1:18-19).

> "But because of your stubbornness and unrepentant heart you are storing up wrath for yourself in the day of wrath and revelation of the righteous judgment of God, who will render to each person according to his deeds: to those who by perseverance in doing good seek for glory and honor and immortality, eternal life; but to those who are selfishly ambitious and do not obey the truth, but obey unrighteousness, wrath and indignation." (Romans 2:5-8).

Yet, because God loves us, He sent His Son to solve our sin problem.

> "Men of Israel, listen to these words: Jesus the Nazarene, a man attested to you by God with miracles and wonders and signs which God performed through Him in your midst, just as you yourselves know—this Man, delivered over by the predetermined plan and foreknowledge of God, you nailed to a cross by the hands of godless men and put Him to death" (Acts 2:22-23).

> "Now the birth of Jesus Christ was as follows: when His mother Mary had been betrothed to Joseph, before they came together, she was found to be with child by the Holy Spirit. And Joseph her husband, being a righteous man and not wanting to disgrace her, planned to send her away secretly. But when he had considered this, behold, an angel of the Lord appeared to him in a dream, saying, 'Joseph, son of David, do not be afraid to take Mary as your wife; for the Child who has been conceived in her is of the Holy Spirit. She will bear a Son; and you shall call His name Jesus, for He will save His people from their sins.' Now all this took place to fulfill what was spoken by the Lord through the prophet: 'Behold, the virgin shall be with child and shall bear a Son, and they shall call His name Immanuel,' which translated means, 'God with us.' And Joseph awoke from his sleep and did as the angel of the Lord commanded him, and took Mary as his

wife, but kept her a virgin until she gave birth to a Son; and he called His name Jesus" (Matthew 1:18-25).

"Have this attitude in yourselves, which was also in Christ Jesus, who, although He existed [be identical] in the form [fully and truly the essence of what something is] of God, did not regard equality [be equivalent, be the same] with God a thing to be grasped, but emptied Himself, taking the form [same as above] of a bond-servant [slave]" (Philippians 2:5-8). [Bracketed portions are the author's.]

He was and is God. (See John 1:1, 3, 14; 5:18; 8:58; 10:33, 38; 14:6-7; 20:28; Hebrews 1:8.)

- » It is difficult to understand, but what all this means is that Jesus Christ was totally God and totally man at the same time.

- » He humbled Himself.

    - » He was born in a stable (Luke 2:6-7).

    - » He had no permanent home (Matthew 8:20).

    - » He rode a donkey into Jerusalem (Mark 11:11; John 12:12-15).

    - » He had to borrow a room to have Passover (Mark 14:12-16).

    - » He was buried in a borrowed tomb, even if it was for only three days (Luke 23:50-54).

    - » He became obedient to the point of death, even death on a cross. Christ suffered not just death but death on a cross—the most excruciating, embarrassing, degrading, painful, and cruel death ever devised (Philippians 2:8).

At no time did our Lord say, "Stop! That is enough!"

- » Not during His trial (Matthew 27:11-14, 24-26, 59-68; Mark 14:53-64; Luke 22:66-71; 23:6-25; John 18:13-24, 28-38).

- » Not when He was mocked (Matthew 27:27-30; Mark 14:65; 15:16-19; Luke 22:66-71; John 19:1-3).

- » Not when He was scourged (Matthew 27:26; Mark 15:15).

- » Not when forced to walk through the city of Jerusalem with a cross on His back (John 19:17).

- » Not when they nailed Him to the cross (Matthew 27:31–35; Mark 15:22-26; Luke 23:33-38; John 19:18).

Christ paid for our sins and saved us from the wrath of God.

> "For while we were still helpless, at the right time Christ died for the ungodly. For one will hardly die for a righteous man; though perhaps for the good man someone would dare even to die. But God demonstrates His own love toward us, in that while we were yet sinners, Christ died for us" (Romans 5:6–8).

> "All of us like sheep have gone astray, each of us has turned to his own way; but the Lord has caused the iniquity of us all to fall on Him" (Isaiah 53:6).

> "Much more then, having now been justified by His blood, we shall be saved from the wrath of God through Him. For if while we were enemies we were reconciled to God through the death of His Son, much more, having been reconciled, we shall be saved by His life. And not only this, but we also exult in God through our Lord Jesus Christ, through whom we have now received the reconciliation" (Romans 5:9–11).

- » Jesus Christ came to earth and lived a sinless life, died on the cross to pay the penalty for our sins, and rose from the grave to purchase a place for us in Heaven.

How do you come to God?

- » God chose, He predestined, according to the kind intention of His will: ". . . just as he chose us in Him before the foundation of the world, that we would be holy and blameless before Him. In love He predestined us to adoption as sons through Jesus Christ to Himself, according to the kind intention of His will," (Ephesians 1:4-5).

- » You came to God by the will of God and not man: "But as many as received Him, to them He gave the right to become children of God, even to those who believed in His name. Who were born not of blood nor the will of the flesh nor the will of man, but of God." (John 1:12-13).

- » God draws you: "No one can come to Me unless the father who sent Me draws him; and I will raise him up on the last day." (John 6:44).

- » God grants you to come: "And He was saying, 'For this reason I have said to you, that no one can come to Me unless it has been granted him from the Father.'" (John 6:65).

- » It was a secure choice: "All that the Father gives Me will come to Me, and the one who comes to Me I will certainly not cast out. ". . . this is the will of Him who sent Me, that of all that He has given Me I lose nothing, but raise it up on the last day." (John 6:37, 39).

- » It is a gift: "But the free gift of God is eternal life in Christ Jesus our Lord" (Romans 6:23).

- » It is not the result of works: "For by grace you have been saved through faith; and that not of yourselves, it is the gift of God; not as a result of works, so that no one may boast" (Ephesians 2:8-9).

- » Accept Christ as Savior. Transfer your trust from what you have been doing to what Christ has done for you on His cross. Trusting Him is what is meant by opening the door to your heart and inviting Him in. "Behold, I stand at the door and knock;…and he with Me" (Revelation 3:20).

- » It involves belief: "They said, 'Believe in the Lord Jesus, and you will be saved'" (Acts 16:31).

- » "But what does it say? 'The word is near you, in your mouth and in your heart'—that is, the word of faith which we are preaching, that if you confess with your mouth Jesus as Lord, and believe in your heart that God raised Him from the dead, you will be saved; for with the heart a person believes, resulting in righteousness, and with the mouth he confesses, resulting in salvation. For the Scripture says, 'Whoever believes in Him will not be disappointed.' For there is no distinction between Jew and Greek; for the same Lord is Lord of all, abounding in riches for all who call on Him; for 'Whoever will call on the name of the Lord will be saved.' How then will they call on Him in whom they have not believed? How will they believe in Him whom they have not heard? And how will they hear without a preacher? How will they preach unless they are sent? Just as it is written, 'How beautiful are the feet of those who bring good news of good things!'" (Romans 10:8-15).

- » Saving faith is not mere head knowledge, like believing certain historical facts. The Bible says the devil believes there is one God, so believing there is one God is not saving faith (James 2:19). Saving faith is not trusting God for temporary crises such as financial, family, or physical needs. Now these are good, and you should trust Christ for these, but they are not saving faith! Saving faith is trusting in Jesus Christ alone for eternal life. It means resting upon Christ alone and what He has done rather than in what you or I have done to get us into heaven.

- » Here is a sample prayer: Dear God, I come to you in the name of Jesus. I acknowledge that I am a sinner, and I am sorry for my sins and the life that I have lived. I need your forgiveness. I believe that your only begotten Son Jesus Christ shed His precious blood on the cross of Calvary and died for my sins, and I am now willing to turn from my sin. I confess Jesus my Lord and believe in my hearts that God raised Jesus from the dead. Amen.

- » When you do and believe these things, you can trust that you are a Christian. "Truly, truly, I say to you, he who believes has eternal life" (John 6:47). "These things I have written to you who believe in the name of the Son of God, so that you may know that you have eternal life" (John 5:13). "But as many as received Him, to them He gave the right to become children of God, even to those who believe in His name, who were born, not of blood nor of the will of the flesh nor of the will of man, but of God" (John 1:12-13).

I would like to clarify a few things as you trust God for your salvation.

- » Salvation is accepting Jesus as your Savior, but it is also recognizing His Lordship. He is the Lord Christ (Acts 1:21; 2:36; 4:33; 7:59; 8:16; 9:17; 10:36; 11:17, 20; 15:11, 26; 16:31; 19:5, 13, 17; 20:21, 24, 35; 21:13; 28:31; Romans 14:9; Philippians 2:11).

- » We are not our own; we have been bought with the price of Christ's death on the cross: "Or do you not know that your body is a temple of the Holy Spirit who is in you, whom you have from God, and that you are not your own? For you have been bought with a price: therefore, glorify God in your body" (1 Corinthians 6:19-20). "You were bought with a price" (1 Corinthians 7:23).

- » We represent Christ as His ambassadors. "Therefore, we are ambassadors for Christ" (2 Corinthians 5:20).

- » Repentance is an important aspect of salvation.
    - » Genuine repentance involves the <u>intellect</u>.
    Repentance is to understand that my sin is an affront to a holy God as well as taking personal responsibility of the actions that I have taken.

    - » Genuine repentance involves the <u>emotions</u>.
    Repentance is not just being sorry (Judas was sorry but was not repentant - Matthew 27:3; the rich young ruler was sorry but was not repentant - Matthew 19:22).
    Repentance is not being sorry for getting caught or sorry for the consequences that your actions caused. Repentance is the anguish at having sinned against a holy God (Psalm 32:5; 51:4).

    - » Genuine repentance involves the <u>will</u>.
    Repentance is not just a change of mind, it constitutes a willingness—more accurately, a determination—to abandon stubborn disobedience and surrender the will to Christ.

    - » Genuine repentance will inevitably result in a change of behavior.

What comes after salvation - Growth in Christ or Sanctification.

- » We are called to work out our sanctification with fear and trembling (Philippians 2:12 - "work" is the normal word for doing labor.) But in the very next verse it tells us that it is God who works in us (Philippians 2:13 "work" is to cause or to energize the work to be done). We do the work but God provides the energy to do that work.

- » Studying God's Word and our praying are part of the sanctification process (1 Timothy 4:5).

- » In Paul's letters we are told to not do certain actions or have certain attitudes (Romans 12:3a, 14:13, 1 Corinthians 5:9, 11, Colossians 3:8-9, 1 Timothy 6:17a).

- » In Paul's letters we are told to do certain actions or have certain attitudes (Romans 13:12b, 14, Ephesians 4:24, 6:10-17, 1 Timothy 6:18).

- » As Christians, we should train ourselves for godliness (1 Timothy 4:7).

- » In Ephesians it tells believers that we should walk (1) in a manner worthy of our calling (4:1), (2) not like the gentiles (4:17), (3) in love (5:2), (4) as children of light (5:8), (5) as wise men (5:15).

- » In Romans 12:1-2 it tells us that we should present our bodies as a living sacrifice.

- » In James 1:22, he tells us to be doers of the word and not just hears of the word.

- » Finally, Peter tells us to be holy as He is holy (1 Peter 1:15).

CHAPTER 1

Information Concerning This Wonderful Book

Proverbs – What a Book!

Proverbs has thirty-one chapters and 915 verses. It has approximately 600 pearls of wisdom that seemingly are not in any order and appear to be like pearls that are unstrung and rolling around on a tabletop. But there are huge benefits when you take those 600 pieces of wisdom and apply them to the events and situations of your life.

Let me assure you, they are not outdated, and they will apply! As a matter of fact, you will be amazed at how much they do apply!

The Outline and Writer of Proverbs

Solomon, son of David, wrote all of Proverbs, except for chapters 30 and 31.

The Introduction: Proverbs 1:1-7

- » 1:1 – The author of the book
- » 1:2-6 – The purpose of the book
- » 1:7 – The theme of the book

Wisdom of Solomon: Proverbs 1:8-29:27

- » 1:8-9:18 – In the first nine chapters of Proverbs, we find fifteen sonnets (short poems) and two monologues.

- » 10:1-22:16 – Addresses wisdom for life issues

- » 22:17-24:34 – Sayings of the wise

- » 25:1-29:27 – Proverbs of Solomon that the men of Hezekiah, king of Judah, copied (25:1)

Wisdom of Agur, son of Jakeh – 30:1-33

Wisdom of King Lemuel – 31:1-31

Ten Statements Concerning Proverbs

These will help you get the correct perspective on this most important and wonderful book.

1. Solomon wrote the Song of Songs when he was a young man. He wrote Proverbs (except for 30 and 31) when he was a middle-aged man. And finally, he wrote Ecclesiastes when he was an old man.

2. The world says, "Live and learn." God says, "Learn and live." The world says, "Seeing is believing." God says, "Believing is seeing." Please, do not go the way of the world, but seek Him so that you can learn, and as you learn, believe and live!

3. Proverbs is a series of short sentences based on God's wisdom. This is key! It doesn't give us man's wisdom, but God's.

4. Do not read Proverbs by itself. Read it in light of the whole of Scripture.

5. You need to read Proverbs with the right perspective. This is written by a dad who loves his sons and daughters, who wants the best for them, and who is crying out for them to follow God and His Word and not their own interests, desires, and passions.

6. If you follow these proverbs, you will become wise and righteous, and your life will be richer and fuller than if you do not follow them. I did not say that you would have an easy life. There is no guarantee for an "easy life" here on earth,

but there is a promise that God will walk with you and strengthen you through your challenges.

7. Proverbs are guidelines to be followed and not mechanical formulas that work whenever you use them. You cannot use them like a subway token that guarantees to open the turnstile every time.

8. Proverbs are procedures we should adhere to, not promises to be claimed. I believe this is the biggest problem with how people use Proverbs today.

9. Do not put God on your timetable. While God's timing is always perfect, it is never predictable, for He is outside of time, He created time, He owns time, and He is not bound by our thoughts concerning time or timing. Keep trusting God, and let Him take care of the timing.

10. Leave a large amount of room for God to surprise you with an outcome that is different from your wisdom and plans. The longer you live, the more you are going to recognize that this is true.

Definitions

These are simple definitions of a few of the words used in Proverbs.

» Knowledge: Facts that are learned through various methods.

» Wisdom: It is more than knowledge. Wisdom is skill, expertise, and competence that understands thoroughly how something really works. It is the complete understanding of a technical or artistic skill (Exodus 28:3; 31:1-11; 35:30–35). It is the ability to make the best and right decisions (1 Kings 3:28).

Wisdom can mean to have the skill (expertise, competence) of a craftsman, sailor, singer, administrator, or counselor. Information is about facts, and knowledge is about fitting related facts together. But wisdom is about using knowledge well. Putting that in a spiritual context, wisdom gives you the ability to live in accordance with the Word of God.

» Instruction: Discipline, correction, training.

» Discernment: To distinguish, to separate, to learn. It is the ability to read between the lines, to distinguish truth from error, right from wrong, good from evil. This quality is invaluable in making decisions.

- » Understanding: Having insights, the ability to perceive past the obvious.

- » Righteousness: An action that embodies and adheres to moral principles and the will of God.

- » Justice: To make right and honorable judgments or settlements.

- » Equity: To make judgments without discrimination.

- » Prudence: This is a good kind of shrewdness. Cautiousness, discretion, foresight.

- » Discretion: The trait of judging wisely and objectively.

- » Naïve: "Naïve ones, will you love being simple-minded?" (Proverbs 1:22). A naïve person is one who is wide open, believes everything (Proverbs 14:15, 18), is easily influenced, is silly, is gullible, is an easy target for someone such as the harlot (Proverbs 7).

- » Scoffers: "Scoffers delight themselves in scoffing" (Proverbs 1:22). A scoffer is a person who has no fear, shame, remorse, or decency. Scoffers can't be corrected. They are an end to themselves. This kind of person is very dangerous. A scoffer is also someone who mocks others or the truth.

Things to Notice about the Book of Proverbs.

Proverbs has contrasts:

- » "But" is used 247 times in Proverbs. Proverbs is written in a very black and white manner without many gray areas. They are bold contrasts. Please do not miss them.

- » Proverbs 10–15 contain 184 verses. 143 of those verses contain the word "but." That's almost 80 percent of the verses! In Proverbs 12, "but" occurs in every verse except 9, 14, and 28. Notice the stark contrast.

PAPA MIKE'S ASSIGNMENT:

Please read chapter 12 of Proverbs and focus on the positive qualities. What three proverbs in this chapter motivate you the most to follow God's ways and Word?

_____

_____

_____

_____

PAPA MIKE'S PRAYER:

Please Lord, help these men and women see the beauty of Your wisdom, and I pray that they never take Your wisdom lightly. Help them not lean on their own understanding or the understanding of their unbelieving friends, but to lean on Your wisdom and Word (Proverbs 3:5-6). I also pray they would learn to go to their parents for wisdom and understanding even if their parents are unbelievers. We can all learn things from those who have lived longer than we have. May they also always seek out godly men and women when there are decisions to be made.

Amen.

Proverbs has connections or completions.

"And" is used 502 times in Proverbs. Connections help you to see a complete picture of a topic. It lets you truly understand what Solomon is writing.

Here are two examples:

> » Wisdom is telling all the ways people ignored her and then shares the result of their actions.

> "Because I called and you refused, I stretched out my hand and no one paid attention; and you neglected all my counsel and did not want my reproof; I will also laugh at your calamity; I will mock when your dread comes, when your dread comes like a storm and your calamity comes like a whirlwind, when distress and anguish come upon you" (Proverbs 1:24-27).

> Go after wisdom, and it will be good for you.

> "Acquire wisdom! Acquire understanding! Do not forget nor turn away from the words of my mouth. 'Do not forsake her, and she will guard you; love her, and she will watch over you'" (Proverbs 4:5-6).

Proverbs has comparisons ("better than" and "like").

Proverbs is filled with beautiful word pictures and vivid imageries. Solomon so wanted to connect with his children. He also wanted to make sure his children understood what he was trying to say.

Solomon uses "better than" twenty-one times in Proverbs.

Nine of the twenty-one verses have to do with money, jewels, great income, and feasting. Solomon is warning his sons to be careful with making riches and income their highest priority. He is making it clear that it should not be—not by a long shot!

Here are a few of the twenty-one verses, so you can see how Solomon uses "better than" in helping you to make to make right choices as well as warning you against the dangers of making wrong choices.

> Wisdom is far better than any riches.

> "For wisdom is better than jewels" (Proverbs 8:11).

> Poverty is better than lacking character.

> "Better to be a poor man than a liar" (Proverbs 19:22).

> "Better is a poor man who walks in his integrity, Than he who is perverse in speech and is a fool" (Proverbs 19:1).

"Like" is used sixty-four times in fifty-four verses in Proverbs. Here are just a few:

> Warning against rejecting wisdom.

> "Because I called and you refused, I stretched out my hand and no one paid attention; and you neglected all my counsel and did not want my reproof; I will also laugh at your calamity; I will mock when your dread comes, when your dread

comes like a storm and your calamity comes like a whirlwind, when distress and anguish come upon you. 'Then they will call on me, but I will not answer; they will seek me diligently but they will not find me" (Proverbs 1:24-28).

> » The life of the righteous.
>
> "The righteous will flourish like the green leaf" (Proverbs 11:28).
>
> » The life of the wicked.
>
> "The way of the wicked is like darkness; they do not know over what they stumble" (Proverbs 4:19).

Proverbs' use of the word "so."

"So" is used thirty-nine times in Proverbs to show you that your choices can have good or bad consequences.

Please take note and then apply that to your own life.

> "Do not let kindness and truth leave you; bind them around your neck, write them on the tablet of your heart. So you will find favor and good repute in the sight of God and man" (Proverbs 3:3-4).
>
> "Like vinegar to the teeth and smoke to the eyes, so is the lazy one to those who send him" (Proverbs 10:26).
>
> "The fear of the Lord leads to life, so that one may sleep satisfied, untouched by evil" (Proverbs 19:23).

Proverbs' use of the word "Lord."

"Lord" is used eighty-seven times in the book of Proverbs.

- » What can we learn about our Lord through these verses?
  - » Fear of Him leads to knowledge (1:7) and wisdom (9:10).
  - » He disciplines and reproves (3:11-12).
  - » He is the Creator (3:19-20; 8:22, 26-31, 20:12; 22:2).
  - » He provides everything (2:6; 10:3, 22; 19:14; sees,).
  - » He knows, sees, and hears everything (5:21; 15:3, 29).

- » He judges everything (3:32-33; 6:16-19; 11:1, 20; 12:2, 22; 15:8, 9, 25, 26; 16:2, 11; 17:3, 15; 20:10, 23, 27; 22:14; 25:22).
- » He rules everything (16:4-9, 33; 19:21; 20:24; 21:1, 30-31).
- » He is the one we should trust (3:5; 16:20; 22:19).
- » He is the one we should honor with our wealth (3:9).
- » He is our confidence (3:26).
- » He is the one we should seek (8:35; 28:5).
- » He is our stronghold (10:29; 18:10).
- » He is the one we should wait on (20:22).
- » Commit your way to Him and He will bring it to pass (16:3).

PAPA MIKE'S ASSIGNMENT:

Please identify three things about the Lord that you did not know before reading this list. Then read the Scriptures associated with that quality. Using those Scriptures, write out what those qualities mean to you.

_____

_____

_____

_____

Now, offer a prayer to the Lord concerning those three things.

A possible reason why Proverbs was written before the major and minor prophets.

I believe God inspired the writing of the book of Proverbs partly as a remedy for the spiritual apostasy of His people, Israel. Oh, if they would have only heeded the Proverbs! God, in His infinite wisdom, knew that His people would need to be reminded again and again regarding how they were to think, speak, and act. So, He inspired the writing of Proverbs to do just that.

The comparison between Job and Proverbs (at the 30,000-foot-level).

Job gives understanding that even if you walk in wisdom or live righteously as Job did, it does not mean you will not suffer.

> "The Lord said to Satan, 'Have you considered My servant Job? For there is no one like him on the earth, a blameless and upright man, fearing God and turning away from evil'" (Job 1:8).

But we know what happened to him:

- » The Sebeans took his oxen and donkeys and killed his servants.
- » Fire from heaven killed his sheep and servants.
- » Chaldeans killed the servants and took the camels.
- » His children were killed by a wind.

The comparison between Psalms and Proverbs (at the 30,000-foot-level).

- » The major focus of Psalms is on man's relationship with God, while the major focus of Proverbs is how man should live here on earth.
- » Psalms focuses on our devotional life, while Proverbs focuses on practical living.

The connection between Ecclesiastes and Proverbs (at the 30,000-foot-level).

Ecclesiastes and Proverbs both help us understand that just walking in wisdom is not the total answer. You must fear and love God as well as walk in wisdom (Ecclesiastes 3:14; 5:7; 8:12–13; 12:13).

The comparison between Song of Solomon and Proverbs (at the 30,000-foot-level).

Proverbs talk a great deal about staying away from the adulteress and the foreign woman, while Song of Solomon shows us the benefit of living with one woman in a beautiful marriage filled with wonderful lovemaking.

PAPA MIKE'S COMMENTS:

Diane asked me this question: "What has the book of Proverbs meant to you personally, and why did you pick this book to write about?"

The more I have gotten involved with biblical counseling, the more I see Proverbs as a foundation of wisdom. It does not have the stories contained in many of the books of the Old Testament or the Gospels, but oh, my heavens, does it contain the Wisdom of God in just a few words. It has taken well over ten years to write this Bible study and, during that time, I have fallen deeply in love with this book and its wisdom.

CHAPTER 2

What David and Solomon Told Their Sons about Living

At the end of David's life, David told his son, Solomon, the following:

"I am going the way of all the earth. Be strong, therefore, and show yourself a man. Keep the charge of the Lord your God, to walk in His ways, to keep His statutes, His commandments, His ordinances, and His testimonies, according to what is written in the Law of Moses, that you may succeed in all that you do and wherever you turn" (1 Kings 2:2-3).

PAPA MIKE'S PRAYER:

Lord, help my children and grandchildren to show themselves to be strong in their faith towards You. Help them to walk in Your ways and pattern their lives according to Your Words. Let them love You with a passionate heart, with all their thoughts, and emotions, and then help them to love others with the same love You have shown to them. Amen.

David and Solomon's Testimonies

David left Solomon a terrible example.

> » He married Michal, Abigail, Aninoam, Mackah, Haggith, Abital, Eglah, and Bathsheba even though he knew it went against God's Word to have more than

one wife (Deuteronomy 17:17). David broke several of the Ten Commandments when he committed adultery with Bathsheba. He put himself above God (Commandment 1), did not honor his or her father and mother (Commandment 5), murdered (Commandment 6), committed adultery (Commandment 7), stole (Commandment 8), lied (Commandment 9), and coveted (Commandment 10).

Solomon left Rehoboam a terrible legacy, even worse than David's example.

> "Now King Solomon loved many foreign women along with the daughter of Pharaoh: Moabite, Ammonite, Edomite, Sidonian, and Hittite women," (1 Kings 11:1-2). Solomon held fast to these in love (1 Kings 11:2). He had seven hundred wives, princesses, and three hundred concubines (1 Kings 11:3), and when he was old, his wives turned his heart away after other gods (1 Kings 11:4). Most of Solomon's wives should have been killed. (Exodus 22:20).

Rehoboam was a very wicked king (1 Kings 14:21-24; 2 Chronicles 12:13-14).

- » Rehoboam was forty-one years old when he began to reign, and he reigned seventeen years in Jerusalem. His mother was a Ammonitess. Rehoboam did evil because he did not set his heart to seek the Lord. Judah did evil in the sight of the Lord, and they provoked God to jealousy more than all that their fathers had done, with the sins which they committed.

Solomon wrote Proverbs to his sons and daughters, but it was also written to all of us.

- » Here's a question: If Solomon messed up with his many wives, why should we pay so much attention to the proverbs he wrote? The answer comes from the fact that the Bible proclaims him to be the wisest man that ever lived. We also know that Proverbs was inspired by God.

PAPA MIKE'S ASSIGNMENT:

I know it is a lot of reading, but I hope you take time to notice what Solomon challenged his sons and daughters to do and why. Each one of these verses contains "My son(s)" or "O son(s)." Please notice the reason why Solomon is crying out to his sons and daughters. [Why?...]

Chapter 1

- » "Hear, my son, your father's instruction and do not forsake your mother's teaching" (v. 8).

- » [Why? They bring honor and beauty to your life (v. 9).]

- » "My son, if sinners entice you, do not consent." (v. 10).

- » [Why? They kill innocent people, and they promise stolen wealth (v. 11–14).]

- » "My son, do not walk in the way of them. Keep your feet from their path" (v. 15).

- » [Why? They will run to evil and shed blood. But in the end they lie in wait for their own blood; and they ambush their own lives (v. 16–19).]

Chapter 2

- » "My son, if you will receive my words and treasure my commandments with in you, Make your ear attentive to wisdom, Incline your heart to understanding; For if you cry for discernment, lift your voice for understanding; If you seek her as silver and search for wisdom as hidden treasure" (v. 1-4).

- » [Why? "Then you will discern the fear of the Lord and discover the knowledge of God" (v. 5).]

Chapter 3

- » "My son, do not forget my teaching, but let your heart keep my commandments" (v. 1).

- » [Why? "For the length of days and years of life and peace they will add to you" (v. 2).]

- » "My son, do not reject the discipline of the Lord or loathe His reproof" (v. 11).

- » [Why? "For whom the Lord loves He reproves, even as a father corrects the son in whom he delights" (v. 12).]

- » "My son, let them not vanish from your sight; keep sound wisdom and discretion" (v. 21).

- » [Why? "So they will be life to your soul and adornment to your neck" (v. 22-26).]

Chapter 4

- » "Hear, O sons, the instruction of a father and give attention" (v.1a).

- » [Why? "That you may gain understanding" (v. 1b).]

- » "Hear, my son, and accept my saying" (v. 10a).

- » [Why? "And the years of your life will be many" (v. 10b).]

- » "My son, give attention to my words; Incline your ears to my sayings. Do not let them depart from your sight; keep them in the midst of your heart" (v. 20-21).

- » [Why? "For they are life to those who find them and health to all their body" (v. 22).]

Chapter 5

- » "My son, give attention to my wisdom, incline your ear to my understanding" (v. 1).

- » [Why? "That you may observe discretion and your lips may reserve knowledge" (vs 2).]

- » "Now then, my sons, listen to me and do not depart from the words of my mouth. Keep your way far from her and do not go near the door of her house" (v. 7-8).

- » [Why? "Or you will give your vigor to others and your years to the cruel one; and strangers will be filled with your strength and your hard-earned goods will go to the house of an alien; and you groan at the final end, when your flesh and body are consumed" (v. 9-11)]

- » "For why should you, my son, be exhilarated with an adulteress and embrace the bosom of a foreigner?" (v. 20).

- » [Why? "For the ways of a man are before the eyes of the Lord, and He watches all his paths. His own iniquities will capture the wicked, and he will be held with the cords of his sin. He will die for lack of instruction, and in the greatness of his folly he will go astray" (v.21-23).]

Chapter 6

- » "My son, if you have become surety for your neighbor, have given a pledge for a stranger, if you have been snared with the words of your mouth, have been caught with the words of your mouth, do this then, my son, and deliver yourself; Since you have come into the hand of your neighbor, go, humble yourself, and importune your neighbor. Give no sleep to your eyes, nor slumber to your eyelids; Deliver yourself like a gazelle from the hunter's hand and like a bird from the hand of the fowler" (v. 1-5)].

- » [Why? From Scripture it does not say, but we are told to do it and that should be enough.]

- » "My son, observe the commandment of your father and do not forsake the teaching of your mother; Bind them continually on your heart; Tie them around your neck" (v. 20-21).

- » [Why? "When you walk about, they will guide you; when you sleep, they will watch over you; and when you awake, they will talk to you" (v. 22).]

Chapter 7

- » "My son, keep my words and treasure my commandments within you. Keep my commandments and live, and my teaching as the apple of your eye. Bind them on your fingers; write them on the tablet of your heart. Say to wisdom, "You are my sister," and call understanding your intimate friend" (v. 1-4).

- » [Why? "That they may keep you from an adulteress, from the foreigner who flatters with her words" (v. 5).]

- » "Now therefore, my son, listen to me, pay attention to the words of my mouth. Do not let your heart turn aside to her ways, do not stray into her paths" (v. 24-25).

- » [Why? "For many are the victims she has cast down, and numerous are all her slain. Her house is the way to Sheol, descending to the chambers of death" (v. 26-27).]

Chapter 8

- » "Now therefore, O sons, listen to me, for blessed are they who keep my ways. Heed instruction and be wise, and do not neglect it" (v. 32-33).

- » [Why? "Blessed is the man who listens to me, watching daily at my gates, waiting at my doorpost" (v. 34).]

Chapter 19

- » "Cease listening, my son, to discipline" (v. 27a).

- » [Why? "And you will stray from the words of knowledge" (v. 27b).] (Solomon is giving a negative example)

Chapter 23

- » "Listen, my son, and be wise" (v. 15a)

- » [Why? "My own heart also well be glad; and my inmost being will rejoice when your lips speak what is right" (v. 15b-16).]

- » "Listen, my son, and be wise, and direct your heart in the way. Do not be with heavy drinkers of wine, Or gluttonous eaters of meat" (v. 19-20).

- » [Why? "For the heavy drinker and the glutton will come to poverty, and drowsiness will clothe one with rags" (v. 21).]

- » "Give me your heart, my son, and let your eyes delight in my ways" (v. 26).

- » [Why? For a harlot is a deep pit and the adulterous woman is a narrow well. Surely she lurks as a robber, and increases the faithless among men" (v. 27-28).]

Chapter 24

- » "My son, eat honey, for it is good, yes, the honey and the comb is sweet to your taste" (v 13).

- » [Why? "Know that wisdom is thus for your soul; If you find it, then there will be a future, and your hope will not be cut off" (v. 14).]

- » "My son, fear the Lord and the king; Do not associate with those who are given to change" (v. 21).

- » [Why? "For their calamity will rise suddenly, and who knows the ruin that comes from both of them" (v. 22).]

Chapter 27

- » "Be wise, my son, and make my heart glad" (v. 11a).

- » [Why? "That I may reply to the one who reproaches me" (v. 11b)]

PAPA MIKE'S ASSIGNMENT:

From theses verses there are seven areas of life that the writers of Proverbs are concerned about for their children. They are pleading with them to:

1. Have a teachable attitude (1:8-9, 3:1-2, 4:1, 4:10, 4:20-22, 5:1-2, 6:20-22, 8:32-34).

2. Be alert to the danger of sinners (1:10-14, 1:15-19, 23:19-21, 24:21-22).

3. Seek after God's wisdom (2:1-5, 3:21-26, 24:13-14).

4. Respond rightly to discipline (3:11-12, 19:27).

5. Avoid, at all costs, all temptation, but especially sexual sin 5:7-11, 5:20-23, 7:1-5, 7:24-27, 23:26-27).

6. Be wise with your money (6:1-5).

7. Be a joy to your dad and mom (23:15-16, 27:11).

Which one of these areas do you think God wants you to grow in the most? What benefits will come to you if you follow His advice?

_____

_____

_____

CHAPTER 3

The Overriding Message of Proverbs

Proverbs 1:1-6

1   The proverbs of Solomon the son of David, king of Israel:

2   to know wisdom and instruction [This will impact our character.],
    to discern the sayings of understanding [This will impact our thinking.],

3   to receive instruction in wise behavior, righteousness, justice, and equity [This will show us how to live.];

4   to give prudence [shrewdness or a good kind of cunning] to the naive, to the youth knowledge and discretion [seeing through something so that you are not tempted] [This will show us how to mature.],

5   A wise man will hear and increase in learning, and a man of understanding will acquire wise counsel,

6   to understand a proverb and a figure, the words of the wise and their riddles [This will impact our listening and thinking.]. [Brackets are the author's.]

PAPA MIKE'S ASSIGNMENT:

The overriding message has to do with being a learner. Why do you think this is important?

_____

_____

_____

Describe the characteristics of a teachable person. List as many as you can. Which of these characteristics describe you? Which of these characteristics should you grow in?

_____

_____

_____

PAPA MIKE'S PRAYER:

I pray that you would take to heart this overriding message of the first six verses of Proverbs! Amen.

PAPA MIKE'S LIFE:

For years I have been getting up at 5:00 a.m. (lately, it seems that it is before 5:00). No, I did not use all that time to study His Word, but I used a significant amount of it. And there is always more to learn. I have studied Proverbs ever since I became a Christian over forty-eight years ago, and I am still learning things. In writing this Bible study, I saw the unbelievably stark contrast between the wise and the fool and the righteous and the wicked.

Please ask God to put a desire into your heart to learn from Christ and His Word (Matthew 11:28-30 - "learn from Me").

I managed people from 1979 until 2015. While at Union Carbide (1975-2002), a missionary at FamilyLife (2002-2007), and the church administrator at The Bible Church (2007-2016), I always tried to hire people who were teachable.

CHAPTER 4

The Five Purposes of the Book of Proverbs

PAPA MIKE'S PRAYER:

Lord, I pray that my family would make these five purposes their life purposes! Amen!

Five Purposes:

1. To know and obey God's wisdom from the heart and the instruction that goes along with that wisdom.

    » "To know wisdom and instruction" (Proverbs 1:2).

    » "Know" means "to know, notice, hear, learn, realize."

    » Wisdom: Wisdom is used forty-eight times in Proverbs.

    » Wisdom is a person: Proverbs 1:20-33; 3:13-18; 4:5-9; 8:1-36; 9:1-12.

    » Jesus Christ is called wisdom: 1 Corinthians 1:24, 30-31.

Instruction: Is used sixteen times in Proverbs.

    » We are to receive, hear, heed, get, and take instructions.

PAPA MIKE'S PRAYER:

Please, God, grow the people who are doing this Bible study in their desires to know and understand Your wisdom and that they will listen and obey its instructions. Amen.

2. To desire discernment and understanding of God's wise sayings.

- » "To discern the sayings of understanding" (Proverbs 1:2).

Discern: To be discerning means that you can distinguish, separate, perceive. It is the ability to read between the lines, to distinguish truth from error, right from wrong, good from evil.

Understanding: Intelligence, insights, skill.

- » Understanding comes from the Lord (2:6)

Benefits of being a man or woman of understanding. He or she will:

- » Discern the fear of the Lord (2:2-5)
- » Be guarded by understanding (2:11; 4:5-6)
- » Be delivered from the way of evil (2:12)
- » Have a fountain of life (16:22)
- » Have a cool spirit (17:27)
- » Find good (19:8)
- » Accept a reproof and gain knowledge (19:25)
- » Be able to draw out what is in the heart of a man (20:5)
- » Establish a home (24:3)

PAPA MIKE'S PRAYER:

I pray that each of you doing this Bible study will set your heart to understand God's Word and His ways and then follow them all the rest of your life. Let them guide you. Amen!

PAPA MIKE'S LIFE:

In May 1975, I graduated with an industrial engineering degree and went to work for Union Carbide in Texas City, Texas. I met some great Christian men who were my age or just a little younger. All of us did well at Union Carbide. In a few years, we were all promoted and, in time, opportunities came to move to other parts of the country. Two of these men moved to Danbury, Connecticut. From a monetary as well as a career perspective, these moves looked very attractive. But in the end, their families suffered. Yes, the same thing might have happened if they would have stayed in Texas, but I believe the choices these men made did not help their families. Soon after that, I was offered a promotion to go to New Orleans as the materials manager of the largest Union Carbide chemical facilities. Diane and I were both concerned with the worldly culture of the New Orleans area. As Diane and I prayed about this decision, we decided that area would not be good for our family. Therefore, I turned the job down. Soon after that, I was offered a promotion as the materials manager in Torrance, California, which I did take. We were able to go to a great church where Diane and I grew in our walk with Christ under the excellent teaching of our pastor there.

Fast forward to 1993, Diane and I were living in West Virginia, and I was offered a job in a purchasing group in Houston, Texas. This group purchased feedstock for our chemical plants. The purchasing agents would buy from the oil and gas industry. That industry was noted for having men who live "unrighteous lifestyles." During the interview process in Houston, a man who worked with me in California (twelve years before) saw me in the hall and asked to speak to me. He currently lived in Danbury, Connecticut, and was down for a one-day meeting (wow … God was at work). He heard I was interviewing for the purchasing job. He asked if I had a minute. We stepped into an office, and he told me he only had one question for me: "Was I as religious as I was when we worked together in California?" I told him I was and maybe even more so. He strongly recommended that I not take the job because he thought my lifestyle would affect my ability to do the job. The manager of the purchasing group knew of my character and beliefs, but he did not think it would affect my ability to do the job. He told me the job was mine, but he totally understood if I turned it down. He also told me if I turned down the job that it would not hurt my ability to get another promotion in the future within Union Carbide.

On the way home, as I was praying and studying God's Word, I found myself in Psalm 1. When I landed in Charlotte, North Carolina, I called Diane. She told me she also read from Psalm 1 that morning. Psalm 1:1–2 says, "How blessed is the man who does not walk in the counsel of the wicked, nor stand in the path of sinners, not sit in the seat of scoffers! But his delight is in the law of the LORD, and in His law he meditates day and night."

I turned down the job. In a few months, Union Carbide offered me another promotion in Houston, which used some of my previous experience and natural abilities. I took the job, and it was good for our family and my career.

"Do not be deceived: 'Bad company corrupts good morals'" (1 Corinthians 15:33).

"He who walks with wise men will be wise; but the companion of fools will suffer harm" (Proverbs 13:20).

3. To receive instructions on how to live righteously, justly, and fairly.

> "To receive instruction in wise behavior, righteousness, justice, and equity" (Proverbs 1:3).

Receive instruction: This word suggests action or response.

- » "In wise behavior" refers to dealing with people.
- » I can't sum up living righteously, justly and fairly any better than what the following verses state:

> "Therefore, we are ambassadors for Christ" (2 Corinthians 5:20).

- » An ambassador faithfully represents the message, methods, and character of the leader who has sent him.
- » He is not free to think, speak, or act independently.
- » Everything he does, every decision he makes, and every interaction he has must be shaped by this one question: "What is the will and plan of the one who sent me?"

> "Be imitators of me, just as I also am of Christ" (1 Corinthians 11:1). (See also Ephesians 5:1–2 and 1 Thessalonians 1:6–7.)

Righteousness: Living free from guilt or sin.

Justice: Have right judgments.

Equity: Living evenhandedly with fairness and no impartiality.

PAPA MIKE'S PRAYER:

God, please increase the desire of the people doing this study to learn from Christ (Matthew 11:28-30). Amen.

PAPA MIKE'S ASSIGNMENT:

In the past six months, what things have you been doing to strive to be more like Christ?

_____
_____
_____
_____

What are you working on now? If nothing, please consider your ways (Haggai 1:5, 7) and identify one righteous thing you would like to incorporate in your life.

_____
_____
_____
_____

4. To establish discretion and purpose in life.

> "To give prudence to the naïve, to the youth knowledge and discretion" (Proverbs 1:4).

Prudence: Craftiness, shrewdness, cleverness from a good perspective and not an evil one.

Naïve: To be open, spacious, and wide. The naive person is wide open, easily influenced.

Knowledge: Knowledge is more than just knowing facts. It is skillfully putting facts into practice.

Discretion: To think through something completely.

Youth: Birth to marrying age.

5. To never stop learning but to learn from the Word of God and not from human reasoning.

> "A wise man will hear and increase in learning, and a man of understanding will acquire wise counsel, to understand a proverb and a figure, the words of the wise and their riddles" (Proverbs 1:5-6).

PAPA MIKE'S PRAYER:

I pray that each of you will read, know, study, meditate, revere, and live in the light of God's wisdom and Word. Amen!

CHAPTER 5

Wisdom Is Shouting

Wisdom is shouting—constantly.

- » Where can a person find wisdom (Proverbs 1:20-21)?
- » Who can benefit from wisdom (Proverbs 1:22)?
- » What do the naïve, the scoffer, and the fool need to do (Proverbs 1:22-23)?
- » How did they respond (Proverbs 1:24-25)?
- » What will wisdom do in the light of their response (Proverbs 1:26-27)?
- » What will they do (Proverbs 1:28)?
- » Why won't wisdom listen to the scoffer (Proverbs 1:29-30)?
- » What is their plight (Proverbs 1:31-32)?
- » What will happen to the one who listens (Proverbs 1:33)?

PAPA MIKE'S LIFE:

I've been amazed to watch God bring Scripture to my life over and over through the years. As I read the Bible consistently, He faithfully brings verses to mind that apply to situations in everyday life.

CHAPTER 6

Walk in the Light of His Word and Wisdom

Proverbs 2:1-22 - Challenges us to walk in the light of His Word and Wisdom.

In Proverbs 2, He is giving you a beautiful picture of personal sanctification [the "if" (in verses 1, 3, 4) / "then" (in verses 5, 9) statements]. Sanctification is the process of becoming more like Christ.

PAPA MIKE'S ASSIGNMENT:

Will you have the right attitude and motivation toward the Word of God (Proverbs 2:1-2)?

_____

_____

Will you pray for the ability to learn how to live the Christian life (Proverbs 2:3)?

_____

_____

Will you have the right determination (Proverbs 2:4)?

If you have these things, then identify the beautiful gifts that you will receive from Proverbs 2:5-19. (There is more than fifteen.)

Identify the benefits of living a righteous life (v. 20-21) and the results of living a wicked life (v. 22).

_____

_____

_____

_____

CHAPTER 7

Human Responsibility and Divine Response

Proverbs 3:1-12 – Human responsibility and divine response.

Before we jump into chapter 3, review the section called "Ten Statements Concerning Proverbs" on pages 24-25. Focus on statements 6, 7, and 8.

Here are two more statements that I would like to make.

- » Proverbs doesn't support "a prosperity gospel"— not by a long shot.

- » Some prosperity gospel followers want to use God for selfish purposes, and I will tell you that is not in God's mind at all. He is a gracious, loving, merciful, and generous God. But He is still God, and He is the one who blesses you. (See more on this in the section about money.)

Be obedient:

- » Human: "My son, do not forget my teaching, but let your heart keep [guard] my commandments" (v. 1). [Brackets are the author's.]

- » God: "For length of days and years of life and peace they will add to you" (v.2).

Be virtuous:

- » Human: "Do not let kindness and truth leave you; bind them around your neck, write them on the tablet of your heart" (v. 3).

- » God: "So you will find favor [grace or good will] and good repute in the sight of God and man [describing Jesus in Luke 2:52]" (v. 4). [Brackets are the author's.]

Trust God and lean not on your own understanding:

- » Human: "Trust in the Lord with all your heart and do not lean on your own understanding. In all your ways acknowledge Him" (v. 5-6).

- » God: "And He will make your paths straight" (v. 6).

Be humble:

- » Human: "Do not be wise in your own eyes; fear the Lord and turn away from evil" (v. 7).

- » God: "It will be healing to your body and refreshment to your bones" (v. 8).

Honor the Lord with everything you have:

- » Human: "Honor the Lord from your wealth and from the first of all your produce" (v.9).

- » God: "So your barns will be filled with plenty and your vats will overflow with new wine" (v. 10).

Accept discipline:

- » Human: "My son, do not reject the discipline of the Lord or loathe His reproof" (v. 11).

- » God: "For whom the Lord loves He reproves, even as a father corrects the son in whom he delights" (v. 12).

- » Note: Love and reproof are different sides of the same coin.

Did you notice how this section began and ended? "My son" (v. 1, 11).

PAPA MIKE'S PRAYER:

Lord, please help those in my future generations to be obedient v. 1), kind and truthful (v. 3), trusting in the Lord and acknowledging Him in everything (v. 5), humble, fearing the Lord, and turning away from evil (v. 7), honoring the Lord with their wealth (v. 9) and, finally, be accepting of the Lord's discipline (v. 11). Amen.

PAPA MIKE'S ASSIGNMENT:

What encouragement did you see in these twelve verses? Did any message spur you on to live a life that's more pleasing to God?

_____
_____
_____
_____

Considering this section, did anything convict you in an area of your life? If so, list that area.

_____
_____
_____
_____

What do these verses say about God?

_____
_____
_____
_____

PAPA MIKE'S LIFE:

Many times, in the past forty plus years, God has encouraged my own heart with Proverbs 3:5-6! These verses have been a tremendous challenge and comfort to me when I didn't understand why something was happening or why something did not happen. They also helped me to keep my sights on Him when a decision had to be made, not on my worldly thoughts.

The time these verses meant the most was when I was in my early fifties. In February 2001, Dow Chemical purchased Union Carbide. It was understood that most middle managers would be laid off. Each of us was assigned a manager in Dow to see if Dow would want us to work for them. I met with my individual one time. The next week he had an issue with his leg that made him very sick. Weeks passed, and most of my friends were told they would not have a job with Dow. But since my contact was sick, I was hearing nothing. I made some inquiries but to no avail.

This is when I started thinking and meditating on Proverbs 3:5-6. Sometimes it would take me over fifteen minutes to go through those two verses:

> "Trust in the Lord with all your heart" (v. 5).

Was I trusting Him to take care of my family and career, or was I trusting in myself or Dow Chemical to do it?

> > Another great verse: Isaiah 26:3-4 "The steadfast of mind You will keep in perfect peace, because he trusts in You. Trust in the Lord forever, for in God the Lord, we have an everlasting Rock."
>
> "And do not lean on your own understanding" (v. 5).

Was I leaning on my heavenly Father, knowing He had this in His hand, or was I leaning on my understanding of what was happening and how it was going to work out?

> "In all your ways acknowledge Him" (v. 6).

Was I acknowledging Him in everything, even if I got laid off?

> "And He will make your paths straight" (v. 6).

Did I believe that He has my path in His hand?

As I meditated on Proverbs 3:5-6, other Scriptures came to my mind which challenged me greatly to trust in the Lord. A lot of these verses declared His sovereignty and extraordinary power.

> "Both riches and honor come from You, and You rule over all, and in Your hand is power and might; and it lies in Your hand to make great and to strengthen everyone" (1 Chronicles 29:12).
>
> "But our God is in the heavens; He does whatever He pleases" (Psalm 115:3).
>
> "The mind of man plans his way, but the Lord directs his steps" (Proverbs 16:9).
>
> "Many plans are in a man's heart, but the counsel of the Lord will stand" (Proverbs 19:21).
>
> "There is no wisdom and no understanding and no counsel against the Lord" (Proverbs 21:30).
>
> "Who is there who speaks and it comes to pass, unless the Lord has commanded it? Is it not from the mouth of the Most High that both good and ill go forth?" (Lamentations 3:37-38).
>
> "For the Lord of hosts has planned, and who can frustrate it? And as for His stretched-out hand, who can turn it back?" (Isaiah 14:27).
>
> "Declaring the end from the beginning, and from ancient times things which have not been done, saying, 'My purpose will be established, and I will accomplish all My good pleasure'" (Isaiah 46:10).
>
> "It is He who changes the times and the epochs; He removes kings and establishes kings; He gives wisdom to wise men and knowledge to men of understanding" (Daniel 2:21).

> "All the inhabitants of the earth are accounted as nothing, but He does according to His will in the host of heaven and among the inhabitants of earth; and no one can ward off His hand or say to Him, 'What have You done?'" (Daniel 4:35).

> "So Pilate said to Him, 'You do not speak to me? Do You not know that I have authority to release You, and I have authority to crucify You?' Jesus answered, 'You would have no authority over Me, unless it had been given you from above; for this reason he who delivered Me to you has the greater sin'" (John 19:10-11).

PAPA MIKE'S COMMENTS:

Here are some more Scriptures that declare the sovereignty of God: Genesis 20:4-5, 50:20; Exodus 3:21-22, 12:35-36, 4:21, 7:3, 10:1, 20,27, 11:10, 14:4; Deuteronomy 2:30, 8:18, 32:39; 1 Chronicles 29:11; 2 Chronicles 20:6; Job 1:12, 42:2; Psalm 22:28, 31:15, 33:11, 75:6-7, 103:19, 139:16; Prov 16:4, 33, 20:24, 21:1, 31; Ecclesiastes 3:14, 7:13; Isaiah 14:24, 43:13, 45:5-7; Jeremiah 32:27; Lamentations 3:37-38; Daniel 4:17; Matthew 19:26 John 1:3-4, 6:35; Romans 8:29, 9:11-15; Philippians 1:6; Ephesians 1:1; Colossians 1:16; 1 Timothy 6:15; Revelations 3:7, 19:6

This is by far the attribute of God that I love the most.

PAPA MIKE'S PRAYER:

I pray that these verses will strengthen your heart to trust and live for Him! Amen.

Back to my story:

Ultimately, my Dow contact had to be admitted to the hospital, and in early April, he passed away. Two weeks later, a new manager was assigned to me. She told me there was little to no chance that I would get a job with Dow. I was scheduled to leave Union Carbide on May 31.

Once again, Proverbs 3:5-6 became my theme song.

During this time, I was turning over my responsibilities of managing the logistics of three worldwide businesses; the one that took more time than the others was the de-icing business. We had 95 percent of the Canadian market and over 65 percent of the US market. I had forty-eight distributions centers throughout North America that my team had to manage.

The people taking over the day-to-day operations were thinking this was just another business. Well, it wasn't. I communicated to Dow's management that if their people didn't get serious about learning how this business operated, they would fail in providing the service which was outlined in each contract. I believed that airports would be shut down, which would be one bad day for Dow.

In mid-May, my Dow manager called me and told me that Dow wanted me to stay on for one year and run the de-icing business. At the end of that time, I could either retire from Union Carbide with a severance package or, if Dow wanted, they could hire me as the logistics manager for the deicing business. I said yes.

In light of the above, I started asking myself and God, "Was working for Dow Chemical all that He wanted me to do for the rest of my life, or was there something different?" Ever since the late '80s, I wanted to be a church administrator in a local church.

The more I prayed, the more I sensed God was leading me to change my career path and do something different, but I had no idea what it was. I also knew that I wanted to get back to the Little Rock area to help Carlee, my sister, with my mom and dad. They were both getting older, and mom's memory was failing.

In October, I called a pastor friend in Little Rock, and he said that he would look around to determine if any church needed a church administrator. In a few weeks, he called and said he did not know of any. But there might be one in a couple of years. He then asked if I would consider joining FamilyLife as a missionary. At first, I said, "No way." My biggest hesitancy was raising support. But the longer I prayed about it, the more willing I became to at least explore the possibilities. I finally called FamilyLife and set up an interview. The interview went well, and it appeared that God was leading me to leave Dow Chemical and join FamilyLife as a missionary.

In February, the battle started raging in my mind. From the world's perspective, this was crazy. I had a great job, I was debt-free, Marcie had one year of college left, and Ben had two. Everything was going well. If Dow chemical did not want me, I could look for another corporate job like my position at Union Carbide. If I became a missionary with FamilyLife, I was going to have to give up an awesome income and benefits and would have to raise support. Ouch!

Once again, this is when Proverbs 3:5–6 became my battle cry.

Later, you will get to hear the "rest of the story."

PART II

TWENTY-FIVE CHARACTER BUILDING PRINCIPLES

CHAPTER 8

Principle #1 – The Fear of the Lord

Please note: You will need to have a Bible with you during this section of the Bible study.

The fear of the Lord – the number one challenge of the book of Proverbs.

The fear of the Lord defined.

Fearing God means to have a reverential awe of God. Reverential awe could be described as an emotion that results in submissive action. It includes respect, dread, admiration, wonder, and amazement for an authority leading to submission. In this case, that authority is God Himself!

PAPA MIKE'S COMMENTS:

I believe that in today's American evangelical church, this concept is not practiced much. I believe we are more focused on God loving and taking care of us, and we do not focus enough on His power, authority, holiness, righteousness, and sovereign rule.

This is something I have been meditating on lately. Maybe you need to grow in fearing the Lord as I did. As you read these next few pages, I pray that God will use His Word and my thoughts to motivate you to develop a healthy "fear of the Lord."

I know this section is long, but it is very important.

What can we learn from Proverbs concerning "fearing the Lord?"

"Fear of the Lord" is used in eighteen verses in Proverbs.

1. It is the beginning of knowledge (1:7).

Knowledge, as used here, is more than an accumulation of information. It involves the ability to view that information with the right perspective and to use it for its proper end.

2. If you don't fear the Lord, you will go your own way and that will not be good for you (1:29-31). This proverb is the only one that has a negative connotation to it.

3. It is a by-product of seeking and searching for wisdom (2:4-5).

4. Live in fear of the Lord and turn away from evil (3:7).

5. Do not let your heart envy sinners, but live in the fear of the Lord (23:17).

6. Fear the Lord and don't associate with those who are given to change (24:21-22).

PAPA MIKE'S COMMENTS:

Please note in each of the last three verses "fear" is a command.

7. Fearing the Lord is better than great treasure (15:16).

PAPA MIKE'S ASSIGNMENT:

Do you believe this verse? Ask yourself this question: Is my dream of the future about pleasing God and being used by Him to further His Kingdom, or is it to get training so I can make good money and acquire possessions?

_____

_____

8. Fear of the Lord is to hate evil (8:13).

PAPA MIKE'S COMMENTS:

Have you ever wondered why you do not hate evil as much as you think you ought or as much as other people? Maybe the real issue has less with hating evil and more with your lack of fearing God.

9. Fear of the Lord is the beginning of wisdom (9:10).

PAPA MIKE'S COMMENTS:

Did you notice Proverbs 9:10 and Proverbs 2:4-5? "The fear of the Lord is the beginning of wisdom" (9:10) and if you search for wisdom, "you will discern the fear of the LORD" (2:4-5).

It is a circle…fearing the Lord will bring wisdom (9:10)…searching for wisdom, you will discern the fear of the Lord (2:4-5).

10. Fear of the Lord prolongs life (10:27).
11. Fear of the Lord leads to life (19:23).
12. Fear of the Lord is the fountain of life (14:27).
13. Fear of the Lord will lead you to walk uprightly (14:2).
14. Fear of the Lord will bring strong confidence and your children will have a place of refuge (14:26).
15. Fear of the Lord is the instruction for wisdom (15:33).
16. Fear of the Lord will help keep you away from evil. (16:6).
17. The reward of humility and the fear of the Lord is riches, honor, and life (22:4).
18. A woman who fears the Lord will be praised (31:30).

PAPA MIKE'S COMMENTS:

Your Dee Dee fears the Lord, and she receives praise from me, her children, and many others.

PAPA MIKE'S ASSIGNMENT:

Read all these verses again, then carefully develop your personal thoughts toward what "fearing the Lord" means to you.

_____

_____

_____

PAPA MIKE'S LIFE:

After studying these verses, I knew I needed to increase my fear of the Lord. Therefore, I started asking God to show me specific ways that would help me in my search to increase my fear of the Lord. The following is the outcome of my quest.

I recognized these things:

1. God is sovereignly ruling and reigning over everything (1 Chronicles 29:12; Job 42:1-2; Psalm 31:15; 33:9-11; 75:7; 139:13, 15-16; Proverbs 21:1; Lamentations 3:37; Daniel 4:17, 35; Amos 4:6-7; Matthew 10:29).

2. God doesn't condone sin and won't overlook it forever.
    - » 185,000 Assyrians died by His hand (2 Kings 19:35-36).
    - » The entire Egyptian army was drowned in the Red Sea (Exodus 14:26-31).
    - » Ananias and Sapphira - death of Ananias (Acts 5:5), death of Sapphira (Acts 5:10-11).

3. No person or thing or any nation can be compared to Him (Isaiah 40:12, 15, 17, 23, 25-26, 28).

4. No one can tell God what He can do or counsel Him. No one has taught Him, and His thoughts and ways are higher than everyone's (Job 42:1-3; Isaiah 40:13-14; 55:8-9).

5. There is nothing too difficult for Him (Genesis 18:14; Jeremiah 32:27; Matthew 19:26; Mark 10:27; Luke 1:37; 18:27).

6. He sees everything (Psalm 139:2-3; Proverbs 15:3).

7. He knows your thoughts and your motives (1 Chronicles 28:9; Psalm 44:21; 139:2-4; Jeremiah 17:10; 1 Corinthians 4:4-5).

8. His goodness surpasses everything that we could possibly hope for or think of (Psalm 136; James 1:17).

9. His holiness is supreme (Leviticus 11:44-45; Isaiah 6:1-3; 1 John 1:5; 1 Peter 1:16; Revelation 4:8-11).

10. We will all give an account to Him (Matthew 12:36).

11. Holiness and the fear of the Lord are linked (2 Corinthians 7:1).

12. Knowing His Word is part of the process of learning the fear of the Lord (Deuteronomy 4:10; 17:18-20; Psalm 112:1).

13. His forgiveness should inspire you to fear the Lord (Psalm 130:3-4).

14. Obedience and fear of the Lord go hand in hand (Deuteronomy 6:1-2; 10:12-13; Ecclesiastes 12:13).

15. Fearing God and working out your salvation go hand in hand (Philippians 2:12-13).

PAPA MIKE'S ASSIGNMENT

Read these fifteen things again. Which reasons compel you to desire to fear the Lord and why? If you are not moved by any of the reasons, then be honest and state what your thoughts are toward God and His Word.

_____

_____

_____

PAPA MIKE'S PRAYER

I pray that each of you will make fearing the Lord a passion for your life. Amen.

CHAPTER 9

Principle # 2 – Love Wisdom and Righteousness / Reject Foolishness and Wickedness

In Proverbs there are four words that are used many times.

- » The word "wicked" is used eighty-four times in eighty-three verses.

- » The word "righteous" is used sixty-six times in sixty-six verses.

- » The word "fool" is used thirty-eight times in thirty-seven verses, "fools" is used twenty-one times in twenty-one verses, and "foolish" is used twelve times in eleven verses for a total of seventy-one times.

- » The word "wise" is used sixty-two times in fifty-eight verses, and "wisely" is used four times in four verses.

- » The wicked and the righteous are contrasted in thirty-seven verses.

- » The fool versus the wise are contrasted in four verses.

When you review these words and the words that describe them, they are describing a believer (righteous and wise) and an unbeliever (wicked and fool). Yes, a Christian can do foolish and wicked things, but they can't live a life of being a fool or being wicked day after day with no remorse. I believe the overall message here is clear. There is a decision to be made, and that decision is: What are you going to do about Christ? Yes, there is a fork in the road, and the path you take will make all the difference in your life.

The righteous contrasted with the wicked:

The righteous

Blessings

- » They will be blessed by the Lord (3:33; 10:6).
- » Their hope is filled with gladness (10:28).
- » They will flourish like a green leaf (11:28).
- » They will sing and rejoice (29:6).

Provision

- » The Lord will provide their food (10:3).
- » They will be prosperous (13:21).
- » They will be satisfied (13:25).

Stability

- » They will not be shaken (10:25, 30; 12:3).
- » Their house will stand (12:7).

Victory

- » They will be delivered from trouble (11:8-9; 12:13).
- » They will not suffer harm (12:21).

Prayers

- » The Lord hears the prayers of the righteous (15:29).

Hope

- » They fall seven times and get up after each fall (24:16).

Words

- » Their words are a fountain of life (10:11).

- » Their words are as choice silver (10:20).
- » Their words are filled with wisdom (10:31).
- » Their words are acceptable (10:32) and true (13:5).

Thoughts and desires

- » Their desire will be granted (10:24).
- » Their desires are good (11:23).
- » Their thoughts are just (12:5).

Relationship with fellow man

- » They will be a guide to their neighbor (12:26).
- » When they increase, the people rejoice (29:2).
- » They are concerned for the rights of the poor (29:7).

Their relationship to their animals

- » They take care of their animals (12:10).

The wicked

Relationship to God

- » They will be cursed by God (3:33).
- » They themselves are an abomination to the Lord (15:9).
- » Their worship is an abomination to the Lord (15:8; 21:27).

Future

- » They will be cut off from the land (2:22).
- » They will stumble or fall (4:19; 11:5; 14:32; 24:16).
- » They will have a name that will rot (10:7).

- » They will be overthrown (12:7).
- » They have no future or any expectations (10:25, 27–28, 30).
- » They will have trouble (11:8; 12:21).
- » They will have wrath as their end (11:23).
- » They will be in need (13:25).

Words and listening

- » They walk and talk with a perverse (6:12) and perverted (10:32) mouth.
- » Their mouth pours forth evil things (15:28).
- » They will not listen to a reproof (9:7).
- » They will be overthrown by their words (11:11).

Relationship to others

- » They are violent (10:6, 11; 21:7), cruel (12:10) and threaten other people (12:6).
- » They rule and people groan (29:2).
- » They have no concern for the poor (29:7).

Heart

- » They have a worthless heart (10:20).

PAPA MIKE'S ASSIGNMENT

Read all these statements again and write one sentence about the righteous person's life. Write one sentence about the wicked person's life. Which results would you like to see in your own life?

_____

_____

_____

_____

The wise contrasted with the fool:

The wise

God honoring qualities:

- » They are teachable (1:5; 18:15; 21:11).

- » They listen to instructions (9:9), reproofs (9:8), counsel (10:8; 12:15), knowledge (10:14), and discipline (13:1).

- » They restrain their lips (10:19) and bring healing to others with their tongue (12:18).

- » They will hold back their temper (29:11).

- » They will be cautious and turn away from evil (14:16).

- » They will not be intoxicated (20:1).

- » They will turn away anger (29:8).

Benefits of this type of behavior:

- » They will inherit honor (3:35).

- » They will make their father glad (10:1; 15:20; 23:15, 24; 27:11).

- » They store up knowledge (10:14).
- » They will be protected by their lips (14:3).
- » They are victorious (21:22).
- » They will be delivered (28:26).
- » They will be a good teacher (15:2, 7).
- » They will control their talk (16:23).
- » They will bring healing with their words (12:18).

The fool

There are three words that are used for the fool (there is overlap in these three words seventy-one times in Proverbs).

They despise wisdom and instruction:

- » Fools despise wisdom and instruction (1:7; 23:9).

His words:

- » He spreads slander (10:18).
- » His mouth will bring him punishment (14:3).
- » He is deceitful (14:8).
- » He spouts folly (15:2).
- » Excellent speech is not fitting for a fool (17:7).
- » His lips bring strife, and his mouth calls for blows (18:6).
- » A fool's mouth is his ruin, and his lips are a snare of his soul (10:14; 18:7).
- » He has perverse speech (19:1).

His relationship with his parents is sad:

- » A foolish son is a grief to his mother (10:1).
- » A fool rejects his father's discipline (15:5).
- » A foolish man despises his mother (15:20).
- » He who sires a fool does so to his sorrow, and the father of a fool has no joy (17:21).
- » A foolish son is a grief to his father and bitterness to her who bore him (17:25).
- » A foolish son is destruction to his father (19:13).

His end is destruction:

- » The complacency of fools destroys them (1:32).
- » A babbling fool will be ruined (10:8, 10, 14).
- » Fools die for lack of understanding (10:21).

Folly and the fool:

- » Fools proclaim folly (12:23).
- » Fools display folly (13:16).
- » Fools feed on their folly (15:14).
- » Fools repeat their folly (26:11).

Other things to know about a fool:

- » A fool hates knowledge (1:22) and displays dishonor (3:35).
- » Doing wickedness is like sport to a fool (10:23).
- » A fool will be a servant to the wise (11:29).
- » Fools think they are right (12:15) and are arrogant and careless (14:16).

- » Fools and evil go hand in hand (13:19).

- » A fool's companion will suffer harm (13:20).

- » A foolish woman tears down her house (14:1).

- » Fools mock at sin (14:9).

- » To a fool, discipline is folly (16:22) and fruitless (17:10).

- » Stay away from a fool at all cost (17:12).

- » A fool does not care about understanding (18:2).

- » Luxury is not fitting for a fool (19:10).

- » A fool will fight and be an irritation to people (20:3).

- » A fool and wisdom do not go together (24:7).

- » Fools will be punished (26:3).

- » Proverbs are worthless to a fool (26:7, 9).

- » Don't hire a fool (26:10).

- » A fool loses his temper (29:11).

PAPA MIKE'S ASSIGNMENT:

Read through both lists. Write two or three sentences concerning the wise.

_____

_____

_____

_____

Write two or three sentences concerning the fool.

_____
_____
_____
_____

Considering your study, what should you do differently with respect to how you are living your life? Be as specific as you can.

_____
_____
_____
_____
_____
_____
_____

CHAPTER 10

Principle #3 – Receive Counsel

PAPA MIKE'S COMMENTS:

Listening carefully and receiving advice or counsel seems to go against most people's thinking. I believe one of the reasons is because people have already made up their minds about what they want to do, and they don't want anything to get in the way of their desires.

Please recognize that you do not have to do what your counselor says. But you do need to receive counsel.

Positive side of receiving counsel:

- » In abundance of counselors, there is victory (11:14; 24:26).
- » A wise man is he who listens to counsel (12:15).
- » Wisdom is with those who receive counsel (13:10).
- » With many counselors, your plans will succeed (15:22).

- » Listen to counsel and accept discipline, that you may be wise the rest of your days (19:20).

- » Prepare plans by consultation (same word as counsel), and make war by wise guidance (20:18).

- » A man's counsel is sweet to his friend (27:9).

PAPA MIKE'S LIFE:

I did not get saved until I was twenty-four years old; before that, I saw little reason to ask anyone for their opinion on any decision that I had to make. Yes, I talked to my dad, but we did not talk much about my decisions or my decision-making process. I am not sure whose fault it was, but I am sure I had a lot to do with it. Very sad!

Please, do not do as your Papa Mike did when I was growing up. I did not know the Bible, and I did not even believe it was the Holy Word of God.

After graduating with a degree in industrial management (combining business and industrial engineering), I started working at Teletype Corporation in Little Rock in December of 1973. Five months later, I decided to go back to the University of Arkansas and get an industrial engineering degree.

That is another God thing I discussed in my testimony (see page 8). I made that decision totally on my own. Praise the Lord, He was directing me even though I did not recognize it at all. I did not know the following verses, but today I love and appreciate them, and I am so glad that my steps were in His hands:

> "The mind of man plans his way, but the Lord directs his steps" (Proverbs 16:9).

> "Man's steps are ordained by the Lord, how then can man understand his way?" (Proverbs 20:24).

> "The steps of a man are established by the Lord, and He delights in his way" (Psalm 37:23).

That decision led me back to the University of Arkansas, where within two months, I met Diane and accepted Jesus Christ as my Lord and Savior. Late in 1974, I started interviewing for jobs. I knew I could go back to Teletype, but I wanted to make sure that was where God wanted me to go. I got an opportunity to visit City Service in Tulsa, Ethyl Corporation in Baton Rouge, and Union Carbide in Texas City, which is below Houston. I got offers from all three and prayed much about my decision. I also asked people at church to pray. By early in 1975, I made the decision to accept Union Carbide's offer.

I graduated in May of 1975 with a degree in industrial engineering and went to work for Union Carbide. In less than fifteen months, I purchased my first brand-new, 1500-square-foot home for $33,400. I once again prayed a lot about it, but I did not know about seeking counsel. It ended up being a great home and investment, but in hindsight, I should have sought counsel.

It was during this same time that I was going to Nassau Bay Baptist Church, where I attended a great singles group. I loved the pastor, Bill Darnell, and his preaching was awesome. We did get to know one another just a little. He decided to leave the church and start a new church with seven men and their families. He made it known that he was not going to open the doors for any additional people to join for at least six months. My heart really wanted Bill to be my pastor. I had already learned so much from him. The more I prayed about it, the more I wanted to be a part of his church. I finally set up a meeting with Bill, and he was thrilled that I wanted to join his church. I was the last person he accepted to join him in this new church.

We started meeting in his home. He got an engineering job to help supplement his income. The second week we met, he told us he wanted all the men to learn New Testament Greek. We met from 5:00 a.m. to 7:00 a.m. every Tuesday for two years. I praise God that he gave me that opportunity.

The next year is when Diane and I got married. Praise the Lord! Diane was a very wise woman, and I have so much appreciated her counsel on many subjects over the past forty-six years.

When we moved to California in 1979, I recognized that I needed men around me who would give me counsel and a discipleship and accountability relationship. It was not long after I moved to California that I met Gary Lorenz. He and I formed a close discipleship and accountability relationship.

God graciously provided good friends with whom I enjoyed discipleship and accountability with each of our moves: 1981 to Charleston, West Virginia: Doug Stinson, Joe Martin, Paul Deakin, and Bud Smith; 1994 to Houston, Texas: Mark Tapp, Mark Mixon, and Rocky Alexander; and 2002 to Little Rock, Arkansas: Mike Davidson, Michael DeLon, Shannon Earls, and others.

I have so much appreciated the wisdom of these men over the past forty years. They have helped me greatly with the decisions that I had to make. Don't ever believe you don't need counsel. God's Word says that we should get counsel, therefore we must need it!

PAPA MIKE'S ASSIGNMENT:

Will you commit to looking for a person who will give you wise counsel as well as being an accountability and discipleship partner? If you think you know someone that might work, will you talk to them about developing this type of relationship?

Write their names below.

_____

_____

_____

_____

PAPA MIKE'S COMMENTS:

Decision-Making – some quick, high-level thoughts:

1. Do not violate biblical commands—the black and white of the Bible—such as "Tell the truth," "Do not commit adultery," "Do not covet," etc.

2. Apply biblical principles (applications of Scripture that are not clear commands).

3. Don't forget to pray for wisdom (James 1:5). Make a list of the pros and cons. But be careful, just because the pros outnumber the cons, that does not mean that you should accept the decision.

4. Get counsel. Find people that you respect who know more than you about the subject that you are exploring.

5. Don't forget your conscience and faith.

> "One person has faith that he may eat all things, but he who is weak eats vegetables only. The one who eats is not to regard with contempt the one who does not eat, and the one who does not eat is not to judge the one who eats, for God as accepted him. One person regards one day above another, another regards every day alike. Each person must be fully convinced in his own mind" (Romans 14:2-3, 5).

> "The faith which you have, have as your own conviction before God. Happy is he who does not condemn himself in what he approves. But he who doubts is condemned if he eats, because his eating is not from faith; and whatever is not from faith is sin" (Romans 14:22-23).

I believe Romans 14:23 is telling you that if you do not have the faith or the confidence to do what you are considering, you should not do it!

One more thing on this topic. If you are married, the person with the tightest conviction should drive the process. Example: should we allow our children to go trick or treating? Let's say that one spouse believes that Halloween is a satanic holiday, therefore their children should not participate in it. The other spouse believes that Halloween is just another day. In light of their two convictions, I would recommend that their children do not participate in trick or treating.

6. Always look beyond the immediate benefits promised by the opportunity. You must weigh the cost of your decisions, not only for the present but also for the future.
7. Never underestimate the impact of a bad decision.
8. Never underestimate the power of your environment (where you live and who you work for and with).
9. If you are married and have a family, don't forget to consider how your decision will impact them.
10. Be careful about only pleasing yourself (Mark 10:45; Philippians 2:3-5).
11. Don't forget that you are a servant of the Most High God.
12. Greater number of choices demands more scrutiny of the choices.
13. After you've sorted through all the considerations in the twelve points listed above, there is a great deal of freedom in what you choose.

PAPA MIKE'S ASSIGNMENT:

The next time you have a significant decision to make, review this list prior to making your decision. Go over your decision-making process with a person wiser and more spiritual than you. Show them the list above and allow them twenty-four hours prior to them sharing their thoughts with you.

Pray much about your decision.

CHAPTER 11

Principle #4 - Guard Your Heart

Proverbs 4:23-26 - This is one of the most important topics that I will discuss. This is where personal sanctification lives or dies.

Get ready. This is a very long section.

Another title for this section could be "Winning the Battle over Sin."
Before I discuss the heart and winning the battle over sin, I must remind you that unless you are a believer in Jesus Christ, you will never be successful in conquering sin. Yes, you might be able to reduce it, but you can't fight sin effectively without having Jesus Christ in your life.

Romans 6 is very clear that believers do not have to sin.

PAPA MIKE'S ASSIGNMENT:

Please read the first seventeen verses of Romans 6 and document the reasons you do not have to sin.

_____

_____

Your Heart:

"In the Bible, the heart refers to the core of your personhood. It is the ruler of your words and behavior; it is the steering wheel of your life; it is what will shape your behavior." – Paul David Tripp.

It is like the motherboard of a computer.

Scripturally, the heart is the immaterial part of a man that contains your thinking, desires, and motivations.

I looked at over 600 of the 900+ references of "the heart" in the Bible. Your heart can be agitated, ambitious, angry, anxious, arrogant, assured, backslidden, bitter, blameless, broken, cheerful, clean, closed, compassionate, condemned, courageous, cunning, deceitful, deceived, despondent, disciplined, discouraged, etc.

Where do desires, lusts, and passions come from (Matthew 15:10-20; 12:34; Mark 7:21-22; Luke 6:45)?

> "But the things that proceed out of the mouth come from the heart, and those defile the man. For out of the heart comes evil thoughts [thinking], murders [acting], adulteries [acting], fornications [acting], thefts [acting], false witness [speaking], slanders [speaking]. These are the things which defile the man; but to eat with unwashed hands does not defile the man" (Matthew 15:18-20). [Brackets are the author's.]

> "For the mouth speaks out of that which fills the heart" (Matthew 12:34; Luke 6:45).

Now, let's look at James 4:1.

> "What is the source of quarrels [wars] and conflicts [little fights] among you? Is not the source your pleasures [desires, passions, or lusts—this is your "wanter"] that wage war [battle] in your members?" [Brackets are the author's.]

Therefore, conflicts don't just happen. They occur because you want something, and you are not getting it or the other person wants something and they are not getting it. Conflicts could be with the individual who is keeping you from getting what you want. Or it could be with a person who has nothing to do with whether you get what you want; but they are there, and you are not happy, therefore they are going to take it out on someone.

When is it wrong to want something? (James 4:2).

> » "You lust and do not have; so you commit murder" (James 4:2a).
> It is wrong when I am willing to sin to get what I want.
>
> » "You are envious and cannot obtain; so you fight and quarrel" (James 4:2b).
> It is wrong when I respond sinfully if I do not get what I want.
>
> » When does a legitimate desire become too important to me?
> When I respond sinfully if I don't get what I want.

A simple way to summarize what I have been saying: "We do what we do because we want what we want."

Here's an example of the heart in action.

When I lived in Charleston, I would wake up in the winter and sometimes there would be ten inches of snow on the ground. We lived on a steep hill that dumped onto a four-lane divided highway.

On this morning, when I saw the snow, I thought of slick streets and that concerned me about my drive to work. Therefore, I got ready and left for work before many people got on the roads. What did I want? I wanted to get to work safely.

Diane saw the snow and experienced the quiet. She then decided to get a cup of coffee, sit by the window, gaze at the snow's beauty, and have a time with the Lord. What did she want? She wanted to experience peace and have a time with the Lord.

When the kids saw the ten inches snow, they would be thrilled because there would be no school. What did they want? They wanted happiness and pleasure.

Key thought: Each of us responded the way we did because of what we wanted! The situation wasn't the real problem; the real problem was those desires in our hearts.

PAPA MIKE'S ASSIGNMENT:

Think about some of your desires." Do they ever cause you trouble or drive you to think or do something that is not the best? Document your thoughts.

_____

_____

_____

_____

A picture is worth a thousand words.

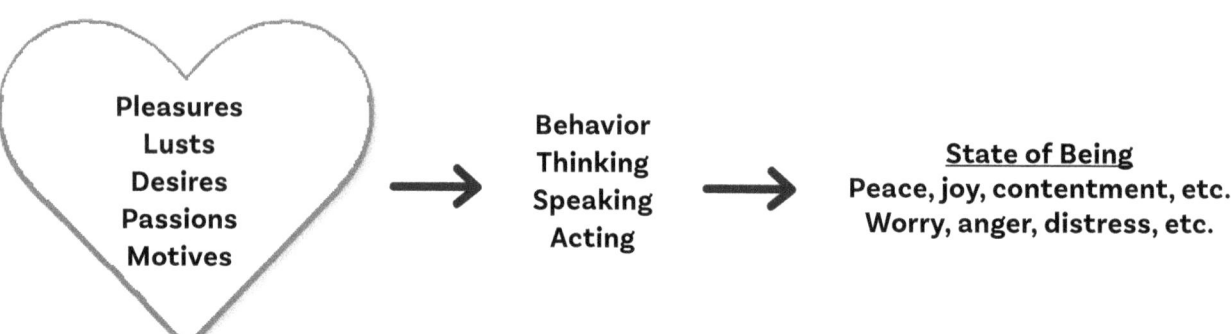

Your thinking, acting, and speaking comes from your heart. They are not just behaviors or what you do. Therefore, just trying to stop a behavior (getting mad, yelling, lying, or spending too much money) will continue unless you deal with the desires, passions, or lusts that are in your heart.

Why should we guard our hearts?

First, God's Word tells us to – Proverbs 4:23.

> "Watch over [command] your heart with all diligence, for from it flow the springs of life." [Brackets are the author's.]

If those desires and lusts are in your heart and not dealt with, you will live out those desires in your behavior. Don't think you can control your behavior without dealing with your heart.

Second, it is the beginning of temptation – James 1:13-15; 1 Corinthians 10:13

- » James 1:13-15:

- » God never tempts anyone:

> "Let no one say [command] when he is tempted, 'I am being tempted by God'; for God cannot be tempted by evil, and He Himself does not tempt anyone" (James 1:13). [Brackets are the author's.]

- » But you are tempted by your own lust:

> "But each one is tempted when he is carried away [lured away or led astray] and enticed [fishing term] by his own lust [same word as in James 4:1-2]" (James 1:14). [Brackets are the author's.]

- » The purpose of temptation is to lead to death (separation):

> "Then when lust has conceived, it gives birth to sin; and when sin is accomplished, it brings forth death" (James 1: 15).

God uses one Greek word, peirazo, to speak of trials and temptations. Trials come upon us from without, and temptations occur within us. But whether you face a trial or a temptation, the decision about how to respond is up to you.

- » James 1:1-4 speaks of trials in your life.

> "James, a bond-servant of God and of the Lord Jesus Christ, to the twelve tribes who are dispersed abroad: Greetings" (James 1:1).

- » Trials will come:

> "Consider [command] it all joy, my brethren, when you encounter various trials [tests or temptations, it comes from the same root word as in James 1:13-14]" (James 1:2). [Brackets are the author's.]

- » The purpose of trials is to produce endurance and to make you mature.

> "Knowing that the testing of your faith produces endurance. And let endurance have its perfect result, so that you may be perfect and complete, lacking in nothing" (James 1:3-4).

For example, suppose a situation happens:

> » It may affect you as a temptation to sin, and if you wrongly respond, the result will be death—separation—from a dream, a relationship, a job, etc.

> » If you see the situation as a trial, and you not only face the trial but work through it, the result will be that you will grow in maturity.

> » Every trial that you encounter becomes an opportunity to endure the trial or to be tempted to sin by wrongly responding. It is up to you to pick which one it will be. But let me make it perfectly clear: the one you pick will influence your life.

One more Scripture which supports James 1:13-15:

> "No temptation [same word as used by James] has overtaken you but such as is common to man; and God is faithful, who will not allow you to be tempted beyond what you are able, but with the temptation will provide the way of escape also, so that you will be able to endure it" (1 Corinthians 10:13). [Brackets are the author's.]

From the Bible, which individuals saw situations as trials and not as temptations?

Job:

> » All his animals and children were killed, and what was his response (Job 1:21-22)?
> » Job got sores all over his body, and what was his response (Job 2:9-10)?

Joseph:

He was sold into slavery by his brothers, put in prison by a lying woman, forgotten by fellow prisoners, but finally became the second-in-command of Egypt. Yet toward the end of his life, he forgave his brothers (Genesis 50:19-21).

Finally, look at the life of Christ in Matthew 4.

> "Then Jesus was led up by the Spirit into the wilderness to be tempted by the devil. And after He had fasted forty days and forty nights, He then became hungry. And the tempter came and said to Him, 'If You are the Son of God, command that these stones become bread.' But He answered and said, 'It is

> written, "Man shall not live on bread alone, but on every word that proceeds out of the mouth of God"'" (Matthew 4:1-4).
>
> "Then the devil took Him into the holy city and had Him stand on the pinnacle of the temple, and said to Him, 'If You are the Son of God, throw Yourself down; for it is written, "He will command His angels concerning You"; and "On their hands they will bear You up, So that You will not strike Your foot against a stone." Jesus said to him, 'On the other hand, it is written, "You shall not put the Lord your God to the test"'" (Matthew 4:5-7).
>
> "Again, the devil took Him to a very high mountain and showed Him all the kingdoms of the world and their glory; and he said to Him, 'All these things I will give You, if You fall down and worship me.' Then Jesus said to him, 'Go, Satan! For it is written, "You shall worship the Lord your God, and serve Him only"'" (Matthew 4:8-10).

I believe Jesus gives us a great clue as to how we should fight sin. We fight sin with the Word of God ["for it is written"]!

Now, let's take what we just learned and apply it to a given situation. Remember, the purpose of this exercise is to help us get to the motives behind our actions. They could be pure and right, or they could be selfish and sinful. But we need to determine what is the "real driver" and then deal with that motive.

Let's say you want a better job.

Next, think through the reason why you want a better job or your "real driver," and then identify the Scriptures that would help you balance the reason from the Word of God.

Possible motive #1 - You want a life where you can purchase the things you want when you want them.

The following Scriptures could help you balance this motive.

Be content: "Not that I speak from want, for I have learned to be content in whatever circumstances I am" (Philippians 4:11).

It is God who gives you your riches: "Both riches and honor come from You, and You rule over all, and in Your hand is power and might; and it lies in Your hand to make great and to strengthen everyone" (1 Chronicles 29:12).

How could these Scriptures affect motive #1?

_____

_____

_____

_____

Possible motive #2 – You want more security for your upcoming retirement years.

What Scriptures could address this motive?

Trust God: "Trust in the Lord with all your heart and do not lean on your own understanding. In all your ways acknowledge Him, and He will make your paths straight" (Proverbs 3:5-6).

Don't put your trust in yourself: "It is better to take refuge in the Lord than to trust in man [in this case, ourselves]" (Psalm 118:8). [Brackets are the author's.]

How could these Scriptures affect motive #2?

_____

_____

_____

_____

Possible motive #3 – You think you deserve it due to your many years of long hours and hard work.

What Scriptures could address that motive?

Work hard because it is the right thing to do: "Whatever you do, do your work heartily, as for the Lord rather than for men" (Colossians 3:23).

God is the one who is behind all promotions: "It is He who changes the times and the epochs; He removes kings and establishes kings; He gives wisdom to wise men and knowledge to men of understanding" (Daniel 2:21).

How could these Scriptures affect motive #3?

_____

_____

_____

_____

Possible motive #4 – You want a life of ease.

What Scriptures could address this motive?

Trials are good for you: "Consider it all joy, my brethren, when you encounter various trials, knowing that the testing of your faith produces endurance. And let endurance have its perfect result, so that you may be perfect and complete, lacking in nothing" (James 1:2-4).

God is trying to mature you: "And we know that God causes all things to work together for good to those who love God, to those who are called according to His purpose. For those whom He foreknew, He also predestined to become conformed to the image of His Son, so that He would be the firstborn among many brethren" (Romans 8:28-29).

How could these Scriptures affect motive #4?

_____

_____

_____

_____

Possible motive #5 – We want to be well-thought-of by other people.

What Scriptures could address this motive?

Be more concerned about what God thinks than any man: "But to me it is a very small thing that I may be examined by you, or by any human court; in fact, I do not even examine myself. For I am conscious of nothing against myself, yet I am not by this acquitted; but the one who examines me is the Lord. Therefore, do not go on passing judgment before the time, but wait until the Lord comes who will both bring to light the things hidden in the darkness and disclose the motives of men's hearts; and then each man's praise will come to him from God" (1 Corinthians 4:3-5).

How could this Scripture affect motive #5?

_____

_____

_____

_____

I hope this exercise has helped you see how to apply Scripture to a desire.

Back to why we should guard our hearts . . .

First (please see page 90): God's Word tells us to – Proverbs 4:23.

Second: It is the beginning of temptation – James 1:13-15; 1 Corinthians 10:13.

Third: A sinful and selfish heart will not only affect our actions, but it will also affect the way we look—Cain—Genesis 4:3-6.

> "So it came about in the course of time that Cain brought an offering to the Lord of the fruit of the ground. Abel, on his part also brought of the firstlings of his flock and of their fat portions. And the Lord had regard for Abel and for his offering; but for Cain and for his offering He had no regard. So, Cain became very angry, and his countenance fell. Then the Lord said to Cain, 'Why are you angry? And why has your countenance fallen?'" (Genesis 4:3-6).

In this case Cain was not getting what he wanted, and it not only showed in his actions, but it showed in his countenance.

Fourth: Older people have taught me, if we live long enough, our thinking will go on vacation and we will just "act out what is in our heart."

That should scare us! Clean up your heart now before it is too late.

When should we guard our hearts?

That is simple! All the time!

> » A lot of us never experience true biblical change because we do not deal with what is in our hearts.

What other tools do we need to do heart surgery?

> » Asking God to help you in examining, searching, and knowing your heart (Psalm 26:2; 139:23-24).
>
> » Studying your own talk (Matthew 12:34; Ephesians 4:29-32).
>
> » Asking people who know you well to help you see your blind spots (Proverbs 24:6; 27:6, 17).
>
> » Identifying when you act in an unbecoming or even in a sinful way, ask yourself why you acted that way.

This is very hard, but it is the beginning of victory.

Another way to ask that question is, "What were you wanting?"

Examples of what you might be wanting:

> » Did you want more pleasure, possessions, power, painless life, better position, etc.?
>
> » Did you want to preserve something—a friendship, job, bank account, relationship, etc.?
>
> » Did you want to avoid something—debt, a reduction in your standard of living, having to confess something, driving in a large city, flying, etc.?

» Be as specific as you can be.

» It will take some time, effort, humility, and honesty.

Once you know what is in your heart, you can then start working on changing your heart's desire.

What else do you need to do to fight sin?

The list is long and not in any order, but I believe these are the things that you need to live out if you are going to be successful in fighting sin on an ongoing basis.

First, be humble (1 Corinthians 10:12; Philippians 3:4-11; James 4:6).

Second, acknowledge your helplessness to do anything good without God (John 15:5).

Third, depend on Him to fight your battles (Ephesians 6:10; 1 John 4:4). Realize that if you are His child, God lives within you. With prayer, knowledge of God's word and a reliance upon His strength, sin can be overcome.

Fourth, see the seriousness of sin—your sin is against God Himself (Psalm 51:4).

Fifth, remember the strong words of Jesus, Paul, and John Owen (Matthew 5:29-30; Romans 13:14; 2 Timothy 2:22).

» John Owen said, "Be killing sin or sin will be killing you!"

Sixth, praise God that He desires you to be sanctified (1 Thessalonians 5:23; 2 Thessalonians 2:13; Hebrews 2:11).

Seventh, realize that God provides the energy for you to work out your sanctification. (Philippians 2:12-13). Note: This was explained on page 20.

Eighth, recognize there are decisions that you must make (Luke 14:28-31; Romans 6; 8:5-13).

Ninth, apply the Word of God to your life (Psalm 119:9-11; Hebrews 4:12).

Tenth, pray that the Spirit would have His way in your life.

Here are four of Paul's prayers. Don't you think we should be praying the same prayers?

> » Ephesians 3:14-21; Philippians 1:9-11; Colossians 1:9-12; 2 Thessalonians 1:11-12

PAPA MIKE'S ASSIGNMENT:

In each of these prayers, Paul uses the words "so that." "So that" is a purpose clause. Now, reread the verses and find each "so that" to see why Paul is praying this prayer.

Eleventh, renew your mind (Romans 12:1-2; 2 Corinthians 10:5; Philippians 4:8; Colossians 3:1-2, 16-17).

Twelfth, stand firm against the schemes of the devil (Ephesians 6:11; James 4:7; 1 Peter 5:8).

Thirteenth, don't reject reproofs or rebukes. [Please see chapter 12 in this Bible study.]

Fourteenth, recognize that your desires, lusts, and passions can become an idol in your life (Ezekiel 14:1-8; Colossians 3:5).

Fifteenth, fight for a good name. It is worth it. (Proverbs 22:1; Ecclesiastes 7:1).

Sixteenth, deal with sin before it "deals with you" (Psalm 32:3-5; 38:3-4).

Seventeenth, hate your sin (Romans 7:15).

Eighteenth, confess and repent (2 Corinthians 7:9-11; 1 John 1:9).

Understand the difference between confession and repentance.

"Confess" comes from two words: "to say" and "the same." When we confess, we are agreeing with God as to what we did wrong. We also understand how we did wrong.

> "If we confess our sins, He is faithful and righteous to forgive us our sins and to cleanse us from all unrighteousness" (1 John 1:9).

> "I now rejoice, not that you were made sorrowful, but that you were made sorrowful to the point of repentance; for you were made sorrowful according to the will of God, so that you might not suffer loss in anything through us. For the

> sorrow that is according to the will of God produces a repentance without regret, leading to salvation, but the sorrow of the world produces death" (2 Corinthians 7:9-10).

"Repentance" means to change your way or mind in light of Scripture. Repentance is a volitional choice towards change. Way to many people get the confessing down but do very little with repentance.

I believe this is one of the main reasons why many people do not grow spiritually.

Seven characteristics of true repentance from 2 Corinthians 7:11.

1. We will do anything to make things right; worldly sorrow will be short-lived and stops short of doing anything to make things right.

    "For behold what earnestness"

2. We want to clear our name totally; worldly sorrow will not be totally honest or open.

    "What vindication of yourselves"

3. We are angry over our sin; worldly sorrow hates being caught and the consequences that follow.

    "What indignation"

4. We have a reverential fear and awe of God; worldly sorrow has a fear of being caught and not being able to practice their sin anymore. [See chapter 5 of this Bible study concerning fear of the Lord.]

    "What fear"

5. We long for all relationships to be restored no matter what it costs; worldly sorrow always has its limits.

    "What longing"

6. We have a zeal for holiness; worldly sorrow always minimizes sin. Most of the time this is lived out by only admitting to partial wrongdoing

    "What zeal"

7. We want to see justice done and we will not cover up sin, but humbly own it; worldly sorrow will always cover up sin and seeks to blame others.

"What avenging of wrong!"

Conclusion: Now we are right with God and have a pure and clean conscience.

"In everything you demonstrated yourselves to be innocent in the matter."

What should we want? What is the ultimate goal of a Christian?

- » To do the will of the Father, just like Jesus (John 4:34; 5:30; 6:38-40)
- » To be pleasing to Him (2 Corinthians 5:9).
- » To abide in Him (John 15:4-5).
- » To imitate God (Ephesians 5:1-2).
- » To follow in His steps (1 Peter 2:21).
- » To give Him glory by:
    - » recognizing we were created by Him, for Him, and for His Glory (Isaiah 43:7)
    - » believing in Him (Romans 4:18-21)
    - » confessing sin (Joshua 7:19-21)
    - » confessing Jesus as Lord (Philippians 2:9-11)
    - » worshipping and thanking Him (Psalm 86:9-13)
    - » loving Him enough to be totally obedient (John 21:18-22)
    - » praying (John 14:13-14)
    - » proclaiming His Word (Galatians 1:22-24)
    - » moral purity (1 Corinthians 6:15-20)
    - » unity (Romans 15:5-7)
    - » aiming our life to glorifying God (1 Corinthians 10:31)
    - » proving to be His disciples (John 15:7-8)
    - » bringing others to Him (2 Corinthians 4:15)
    - » building up the downtrodden (Isaiah 61:1-3)
    - » completing the work that God has given us to do (John 17:4)

- » doing good works and those good works are seen by men (Matthew 5:14-16)
- » giving to the Lord's work (the people who receive our gifts will glorify God) (2 Corinthians 9:10-15)

PAPA MIKE'S LIFE:

During the 1980s, while I was working at Union Carbide, I desired recognition in the form of high-performance ratings. Some of this was because higher ratings led to a promotion and to higher salaries. When I did not get the recognition, I felt I deserved, I had my own little pity party. I knew in my heart that was not the best; finally, I started confessing those desires for recognition. But I didn't see how destructive those desires could be—a loss of inner joy!

I continued to struggle with this; but then I started looking for Scriptures that would help.

"Whatever you do in word or deed, do all in the name of the Lord Jesus, giving thanks through Him to God the Father" (Colossians 3:17).

"Slaves, be obedient to those who are your masters [your boss] according to the flesh, with fear and trembling, in the sincerity of your heart, as to Christ; not by way of eye-service, as men-pleasers, but as slaves of Christ, doing the will of God from the heart" (Ephesians 6:5-6).

"Slaves, in all things obey those who are your masters on earth, not with external service, as those who merely please men, but with sincerity of heart, fearing the Lord. Whatever you do, do your work heartily, as for the Lord rather than for men, knowing that from the Lord you will receive the reward of the inheritance. It is the Lord Christ whom you serve" (Colossians 3:22-24).

I decided that I wanted to work for God and not man. And this helped, but not completely.

Later, I recognized I was still wanting recognition for the things that I did. And that is when I started digging deeper into my heart and thinking through more Scriptures that could be applied to my problem. That is when it hit me: Did I want my reward now or later?

Righteousness: "Beware of practicing your righteousness before men to be noticed by them; otherwise you have no reward with your Father who is in heaven" (Matthew 6:1).

Giving: "But when you give to the poor, do not let your left hand know what your right hand is doing, so that your giving will be in secret; and your Father who sees what is done in secret will reward you" (Matthew 6:3-4).

Praying: "But you, when you pray, go into your inner room, close your door and pray to your Father who is in secret, and your Father who sees what is done in secret will reward you" (Matthew 6:6).

Fasting: "But you, when you fast, anoint your head and wash your face so that your fasting will not be noticed by men, but by your Father who is in secret; and your Father who sees what is done in secret will reward you" (Matthew 6:17-18).

I had to work for God and not man. I had to want my reward in heaven and not on this earth.

But God was not through with me yet. I was convicted afresh by His Word (Hebrews 4:12).

- » Paul calls himself a "bond-servant" or "slave" (Romans 1:1; Philippians 1:1; Titus 1:1).
- » Simeon was a bond-servant (Luke 2:29).
- » Jesus was a bond-servant (Philippians 2:7).
- » Epaphras was a bond-servant (Colossians 1:7).
- » Tychicus was a bond-servant (Colossians 4:7).
- » James was a bond-servant (James 1:1).
- » Peter was a bond-servant (2 Peter 1:1).
- » Jude was a bond-servant (Jude 1).

The Gospels mention the same concept regarding our personal relationships and being a bond-slave.

> "Calling them to Himself, Jesus said to them, 'You know that those who are recognized as rulers of the Gentiles lord it over them; and their great men exercise authority over them. But it is not this way among you, but whoever wishes to become great among you shall be your servant; and whoever wishes to be first among you shall be slave of all. For even the Son of Man did not come to be served, but to serve, and to give His life a ransom for many'" (Mark 10:42-45).

> "So when He had washed their feet, and taken His garments and reclined at the table again, He said to them, 'Do you know what I have done to you? You call Me Teacher and Lord; and you are right, for so I am. If I then, the Lord and the Teacher, washed your feet, you also ought to wash one another's feet. For I gave you an example that you also should do as I did to you. Truly, truly, I say to you, a slave is not greater than his master, nor is one who is sent greater than the one who sent him. If you know these things, you are blessed if you do them." (John 13:12-17).

He wanted me to think like a slave! Maybe a better way would be for me to act like a slave. I am not going to say that I never have those thoughts concerning desiring recognition, but they are a lot less than they were in the past. If I have those thoughts, I remember quickly:

- » I must work for God and not man.

- » I must want my reward in heaven and not on this earth.

- » I must live like a bond-slave.

PAPA MIKE'S ASSIGNMENT:

What have you learned from this chapter? What do you need to do differently?

_____

_____

_____

CHAPTER 12

Principle #5 – Be Open to Reproofs and Rebukes

God's Word teaches you to be open to reproofs and rebukes.

- » "Turn to my reproof, behold, I will pour out my spirit on you; I will make my words known to you" (1:23).

- » "A fool rejects his father's discipline, but he who regards reproof is sensible" (15:5).

- » "He whose ear listens to the life-giving reproof will dwell among the wise" (15:31).

- » "A rebuke goes deeper into one who has understanding than a hundred blows into a fool" (17:10).

Reproofs can be refused, ignored, neglected, or not wanted.

- » "Because I [wisdom] called and you refused" (1:24). [Brackets are the author's.]

- » "I [wisdom] stretched out my hand and no one paid attention" (1:24). [Brackets are the author's.]

- » "And you neglected all my [wisdom] counsel" (1:25). [Brackets are the author's.]

- » "And did not want my [wisdom] reproof (1:25). [Brackets are the author's.]

What does Hebrews 12:5-6 tell us concerning how we should react to reproofs?

Ignoring, rejecting, or hating reproofs is not wise.

- » "They spurned all my reproof. So they shall eat the fruit of their own way and be satiated with their devices" (1:30-31).

- » "He who ignores reproof goes astray" (10:17).

- » "He who hates reproof is stupid" (12:1).

- » "He who hates reproof will die" (15:10).

- » "A man who hardens his neck after much reproof will suddenly be broken beyond remedy" (29:1).

PAPA MIKE'S ASSIGNMENT:

I know this is hard, but honestly ask yourself this question: Do you want to be wise and sensible (regard reproofs) or do you want to be a fool or stupid (reject reproofs)?

_____

_____

_____

_____

PAPA MIKE'S LIFE:

I have been blessed by having men in my life who would not allow me to act or do things that were not the best. They would ask me lots of questions concerning my thinking, words, or actions to make me think about my life. I did not always like their questions, but their questions were right-on, and they helped me to keep living for Christ.

While I was the chairman of the elders, I assembled a list of accountability questions. The following is that list. Once a year, I had all the elders at BCLR review and discuss the questions that they needed to work on.

- How is your relationship with God?
- How are your quiet times?
- On average, how many days each week do you open God's Word?
- How many days a week do you pray by yourself?
- How have you fought for holiness in your life?
- Where have you seen the Lord at work this year?
- What has the Lord been teaching you this year?
- Where have you been convicted the most?
- What prayers have you seen God answer?
- Have you been with a member of the opposite sex in a way that might be considered compromising or questionable?
- Have you had any financial dealings that lack integrity?
- Have you given proper time to your wife and kids?
- Have you exposed yourself to any sexually explicit material?
- Have you taken care of your body?
- How is your giving to the church?
- What are the biggest barriers to your relationship with your wife?

- » What are the biggest barriers to your relationship with your children?

- » What are the most serious temptations you face at home? Work? Elsewhere?

- » If Satan were to wage an all-out attack on your life, what area(s) would he focus on? What are your greatest points of vulnerability (e.g., sexual impurity, financial irresponsibility, dishonesty, greed, pride, etc.)?

- » What happened this year that put you to the test? How did you respond?

- » Have you been living within your means?

- » Have you battled against ungodly thoughts (e.g., bitterness, resentment, lust, pride, jealously, covetousness, racism, etc.)?

- » Have you resisted any ongoing temptations?

- » Have you resisted pride?

- » Have you cultivated humility?

- » Have you dealt with any of the following issues in a constructive manner: anger, slothfulness, passivity, gluttony, speech, etc.?

- » How are you doing in your relationships at work or school?

- » How are you doing with your thought life?

- » What kind of ministry did you have this week?

- » Have you consistently led your wife and children in family devotions or worship?

- » Do you have any unreconciled relationships either within your church or with those outside the church?

PAPA MIKE'S PRAYER:

I pray that you will look for men and women who will hold you accountable for your thinking, words, and actions and that you will desire and accept their reproofs and rebukes. Amen.

PAPA MIKE'S LIFE:

My sons and I backpacked many times between the years they were in grade school, high school, and even into their college years. Many times, we went on two backpacks per year—one in the spring and another in the fall. A couple of times, we even went over Christmas break. Some of my fondest memories with my sons were those backpacking trips. My closest and best friend, Mick Spena, and his son, Matt, accompanied us on most of those trips. Besides being a great time to get away from the hustle and bustle of everyday life, it was also a great time to enjoy God's creation and our friendships.

The trail we hiked most was the Ozark Highland Trail in northwest Arkansas. The trail ran from Fort Smith to the Buffalo River, which is approximately 160 miles. We hiked all of it except the first section from Fort Smith, which is approximately twenty miles. We hiked some sections many times.

The trail was stunning as it rambled through the Ozark Mountains. We always camped by streams. It was so nice to wake up in the night and listen to the water in the nearby stream. We would start each hike at one spot and either head east or west. We would hike approximately forty-five to fifty-five miles in five to six days.

One aspect of our backpacking trips can be applied spiritually. The way we knew we were on the Ozark Highland Trail was that every so often there would be a blue blaze on a tree beside the trail. That blaze would tell us we were still on the trail. If we did not see a blaze for a while, we would stop and go back until we found a blue blaze, and then we would start again looking for the next blue blaze. It would not be long before we would see another blue blaze, and our hearts would be glad.

Now, how can that be applied to a person's spiritual life? The Word of God can guide you to walk on the right path, but ignoring the Word of God can lead to much trouble. Therefore, just like we had to watch for the blue blazes on the Ozark Highland Trail or we found ourselves off the trail and lost, we need to look at the Word of God so we don't get off the path God would have us walk.

Please notice the eight things this father wants his son to do from Proverbs 4:20-27.

"My son,"

- » (1) "Give attention to my words" (v. 20).
- » (2) "Incline your ear to my sayings" (v. 20).
- » (3) "Do not let them depart from your sight; keep them in the midst of your heart. For they are life to those who find them and health to all their body" (v. 21-22).
- » (4) "Watch over your heart with all diligence, for from it flow the springs of life" (v. 23).
- » (5) "Put away from you a deceitful mouth and put devious speech far from you" (v. 24).
- » (6) "Let your eyes look directly ahead and let your gaze be fixed straight in front of you" (v. 25).
- » (7) "Watch the path of your feet and all your ways will be established. Do not turn to the right nor to the left" (v. 26-27a).
- » (8) "Turn your foot from evil" (v. 27b).

PAPA MIKE'S PRAYER:

Lord, I pray that my descendants will be men and women who will love You with all their hearts, minds, and strength, and delight in Your Word and obey it. I pray that You will show them when they have drifted from You and Your truth and that they will respond to Your promptings by getting back into Your Word and obeying it. Amen.

> "Open my eyes, that I may behold wonderful things from Your law" (Psalm 119:18).

CHAPTER 13

Principle #6 – Be Careful How and Where You Walk as Well as Whom You Walk With

Some thoughts on "walking" from Ephesians.

- » Walk in His good works (2:10)

- » Walk worthy (4:1)

- » Walk not as the Gentiles walk (4:17)

- » Walk in love (5:2)

- » Walk in the light (5:8)

- » Walk in wisdom (5:15)

Thoughts on being careful.

- » Stay away from sinners (Proverbs 1:10), and wicked and evil men (Proverbs 4:14).

- » Remember that bad company corrupts good morals (1 Corinthians 15:33).

- Stay away from sexually immoral people (Proverbs 2:16-19; 5:3-6, 20; 6:24-29; 7:4-5, 24-27; 9:13-18).

- Listen to wisdom (Proverbs 3:21-23).

- Listen to your mom and dad (Proverbs 4:10-12; 6:20-22).

- Walk with wise men (Proverbs 13:20).

- Walk in the fear of the Lord (Proverbs 14:2).

- Be cautious (Proverbs 14:15-16; 22:3).

- Desire understanding (Proverbs 15:21).

- Don't associate with a man of violence (Proverbs 16:29) or an angry man (Proverbs 22:24-25).

- Don't associate with gossips (Proverbs 20:19).

- Don't be envious of sinners (Proverbs 23:17) or evil men (Proverbs 24:1).

- Stay away from heavy drinkers or gluttons (Proverbs 23:20-21).

- Walk blamelessly (Proverbs 28:18, 26).

- Don't be a partner with a thief (Proverbs 29:24).

PAPA MIKE'S COMMENTS:

When Proverbs tells us not to associate with these people, it is warning us not to become best friends with them. It doesn't mean you can't speak to them or show love to them.

PAPA MIKE'S ASSIGNMENT:

Where have you been in the past few weeks? Are these good places to be visiting?

_____

_____

_____

_____

Who have you been with in the past few weeks? Are these good people to associate with?

_____

_____

_____

_____

PAPA MIKE'S PRAYER:

Lord, I pray that You will take Your Word and put it into the hearts of the people who are doing this Bible study. I pray that they will desire to walk with Christ and not in the way of the world. May they become children of the light so people can see the difference that Christ makes. Amen!

CHAPTER 14

Principle #7 – Accept God's Discipline and Be Obedient

I know some of these verses apply to parents disciplining their children, but I believe you can learn something from them. I pray that many of you will be parents in the future.

The book of Proverbs on discipline:

- » Discipline and love are two sides of the same coin, and it takes both to train us (3:11-12).

- » Discipline is the way to life (Proverbs 6:23).

- » Discipline proves that the person who is disciplining you loves you (13:24).

- » Discipline should be done early in a child's life (19:18).

- » Accept discipline that you may be wise (19:20)

- » Cease listening to discipline, and you will stray from the words of knowledge (19:27).

- » Discipline will remove foolishness (22:15).

- » Discipline will not cause death but will rescue you (23:13-14).

- » Discipline will give wisdom (29:15).

- » Discipline your son and daughter, and they will give you comfort (29:17).

PAPA MIKE'S COMMENTS:

The topic of discipline is not just for the child.

Discipline can come from the government (speeding tickets or jail time for stealing, etc.), bosses (reprimands and being fired), leaders of the church (being corrected due to straying from the truth or being disciplined out of the church), and civic organizations (excluded from certain activities or being expelled).

But I will challenge you that the best form of discipline is "self-discipline." You might ask why I say that.

You are the best one to avoid getting a ticket for speeding, not getting fired by your boss, not being disciplined by the church, or not being expelled from a civic organization. But I will tell you that being self-disciplined is not easy.

- » You first must recognize that you need self-discipline.

- » Second, you need to identify the area(s) in which you need to be self-disciplined.

- » Third, you need to pray and ask the Holy Spirit to strengthen you for the battle ahead.

- » Fourth, you need to identify just how you are going to be self-disciplined.

- » And finally, you need to have someone help you to stay the course because, for a lot of us, self-discipline does not come easy; we can grow weary and possibly give up.

A few years ago, Ben, my son, asked me to develop a list of spiritual items that would be a good starting point for being disciplined in his Christian life. The following is the list I gave Ben.

Note: Only start with one or two and as you get those working, then add one or two more.

- » Have a quiet time MOST mornings (Psalm 1; John 15).

- » Pray daily, even if it is only for a few minutes (1 Thessalonians 5:17).

- » Walk in love. Ask yourself: What would love require of me today? (John 13:5-17; 1 Corinthians 13:4-8; Ephesians 5:2; Philippians 2:3; 1 John 3:16-17)? Do at least one loving action each day.

- » Watch your heart with all diligence. Confess sinful thoughts and actions (Proverbs 4:23; Matthew 12:34; 15:10-20; James 4:1-3).

- » Set your affections on things above (Colossians 3:1-3).

- » Deal with temptations before they deal with you (Genesis 4:1-16 [especially 4:5-6]; Psalm 32:1-5; 38:1-4; 51:1-4; James 1:13-16).

- » Be humble and not prideful. Confess prideful thoughts, attitudes, and actions (Proverbs 18:12; 22:4; 29:23; 16:5; 8:13; Matthew 20:25-28; Mark 10:42-45; Luke 22:25-27; James 4:6, 10; 1 Peter 5:5-6).

- » Be thankful. At the end of the day, list a few things you are thankful for (Colossians 3:17; 1 Thessalonians 5:18).

- » Be forgiving (Ephesians 4:32; Colossians 3:13).

- » Be careful with your words (Proverbs 18:21; Ephesians 4:29). (Note: cross-reference the following in Proverbs: "word(s)," "lip(s)," "mouth.")

PAPA MIKE'S ASSIGNMENT:

Which one of the above items do you plan to implement this week? What are your points of action?

_____

_____

_____

_____

Obedience

- » Obedience will bring peace, life, and health (Proverbs 3:1-2; 4:4, 20-22; 7:1-2; 16:17).

- » Obedience will bring guidance, sweet sleep, and instruction (Proverbs 6:20-22).

PAPA MIKE'S PRAYER:

May the Lord burden your heart to be obedient to His Word. May you have a heart to obey because you love God, and it's the right thing to do, not just because it will help you live a better life. Amen!

CHAPTER 15

Principle # 8 – How to Deal with Temptation

Sexual temptation

Please notice that this father is pleading.

> "My son, give attention [command] to my wisdom, incline [command] your ear to my understanding; that you may observe discretion and your lips may reserve knowledge. For the lips of an adulteress drip honey and smoother than oil is her speech; but in the end she is bitter as wormwood, sharp as a two-edged sword. Her feet go down to death, her steps take hold of Sheol" (Proverbs 5:1-5). [Brackets are the author's.]

> "Now then, my sons, listen [command] to me and do not depart from the words of my mouth. Keep [command] your way far from her and do not go near the door of her house, or you will give your vigor to others and your years to the cruel one" (Proverbs 5:7-9). [Brackets are the author's.]

> "For why should you, my son, be exhilarated with an adulteress and embrace the bosom of a foreigner?" (Proverbs 5:20).

"My son, observe [command] the commandment of your father and do not forsake the teaching of your mother; bind [command] them continually on your heart; tie [command] them around your neck" (Proverbs 6:20-21).

"To keep you from the evil woman, from the smooth tongue of the adulteress. Do not desire her beauty in your heart, nor let her capture you with her eyelids. For on account of a harlot one is reduced to a loaf of bread, and an adulteress hunts for the precious life" (Proverbs 6:24-26).

"The one who commits adultery with a woman is lacking sense; he who would destroy himself does it. Wounds and disgrace he will find, and his reproach will not be blotted out" (Proverbs 6:32-33).

"My son, keep [command] my words and treasure my commandments within you. Keep [command] my commandments and live [command], and my teaching as the apple of your eye. Bind them [command] on your fingers; write them [command] on the tablet of your heart. Say [command] to wisdom, 'You are my sister,' and call understanding your intimate friend; that they may keep you from an adulteress, from the foreigner who flatters with her words" (Proverbs 7:1-5). [Brackets are the author's.]

"Suddenly he follows her as an ox goes to the slaughter, or as one in fetters to the discipline of a fool, until an arrow pierces through his liver; as a bird hastens to the snare, so he does not know that it will cost him his life" (Proverbs 7:22-23).

"Now therefore, my sons, listen [command] to me, and pay attention [command] to the words of my mouth. Do not let your heart turn aside to her ways, do not stray into her paths. For many are the victims she has cast down, and numerous are all her slain. Her house is the way to Sheol, descending to the chambers of death" (Proverbs 7:24-27). [Brackets are the author's.]

Give [command] me your heart, my son, and let your eyes delight in my ways. For a harlot is a deep pit and an adulterous woman is a narrow well. Surely, she lurks as a robber, and increases the faithless among men" (Proverbs 23:26-28). [Brackets are the author's.]

PAPA MIKE'S LIFE:

While at Union Carbide, I took frequent business trips. Along the way, I started watching shows I would not have watched with my family. I was eventually convicted of this. I tried not to watch those shows, but some nights I did not keep my commitments. Therefore, I decided I needed to do something else. So, I came up with the commitment to not watch TV when I was on any business trip. I also decided I needed accountability for my actions. So, I told my accountability partner that after each business trip, I would email him if I had failed in my commitment to not watch TV. I was on a business trip in Midland, Michigan, on 9/11. I called Diane and asked her if I could watch the news. She told me that would be fine. No other time did I watch TV while on a business trip. I am not sure what helped me keep my commitment. Was it "self-discipline," or was it the fact that if I did fail, I would have to tell my accountability partner? Well, I really don't care which one it was. I am thrilled I never failed again in that commitment.

PAPA MIKE'S COMMENTS:

I have counseled several men who have been addicted to pornography. Praise the Lord, I have seen God work in men's lives, even though they have been participating in this addiction for over fifteen years. The following were things I believe helped these men to find freedom from pornography:

1. Understanding this activity was sin (Matthew 5:27-28).

2. Understanding this activity was a sin against God (Psalm 51:4).

3. It was taking a toll on them (Psalm 32:3-4).

4. Confession was part of the solution (Psalm 32:5; 1 John 1:9).

5. But confession was not enough. They had to learn what true repentance was and then honestly repent (see pages 100-101; 2 Corinthians 7:11).

6. The Word of God was part of the solution to them finding victory (Hebrews 4:12).

7. They found Scriptures to memorize to help them in fighting this temptation (see pages 92-96; Job 31:1; James 1:13-15).

8. Prayer was part of the solution (Hebrews 4:14-16).

9. Once they started sharing about this addiction, they realized that this "private sin" was affecting others, especially their wives. We never sin in a vacuum. Our sin always affects others.

10. They realized they could not fight this alone; they needed an accountability partner (Galatians 6:1-2).

11. They learned to flee from youthful lust (2 Timothy 2:22).

12. In all this, they learned that God was the center of their victory (John 15:1-11).

13. I had them read, *Finally Free* by Heath Lambert.

PAPA MIKE'S PRAYER:

Please, Lord God, protect my relatives from going to an adulteress. No matter how good it looks, You have promised that its end is destruction. Amen.

Excessive indulgence in wine, mixed wine, or food - Proverbs 23:19-21, 29-35

PAPA MIKE'S LIFE:

Prior to getting saved when I was twenty-four years old, I did drink, and sometimes too much. I can honestly tell you, at that time, I thought it was fun. But now that I have lived over forty-nine years without drinking alcohol, it was not as fun as I thought it was—not by a long shot! As a matter of fact, it was extremely foolish. I praise the Lord that He protected me and the other people in my car and other cars on the road. I know one man who killed a person while driving drunk, and he lives with it to this day. Please, do not drink and drive. Please do not drink to excess. I will testify from my experience that not drinking is far more fulfilling than drinking!

PAPA MIKE'S PRAYER:

Lord, burden these people to be filled with the Spirit (Ephesians 5:18) and not to be drunk with alcoholic beverages or high on drugs. Amen.

CHAPTER 16

Principle #9 – How to Handle Money

Before we learn what Proverbs has to say about money, I would like to share several things I have learned concerning money.

Money has been called the substance that can buy us everything but inner peace and happiness and can take us anywhere but heaven.

What are some things money can't buy?

- » It may buy you a stack of books and pay your tuition to the finest university, but it can't buy the ability to learn.

- » It may buy you medicines and doctors, but it can't buy you health.

- » It may buy you a million-dollar house with an ocean view, but it can't buy a "home."

- » It may buy you companionship, but it can't buy a "true friend."

- » It may buy you a solid-gold crucifix, but it can't buy a Savior.

Let's start with a few questions:

How important are money and possessions to God?

- » Jesus told thirty-eight parables in the Gospels. Out of those thirty-eight, sixteen dealt with money and possessions.

- » Christ said more about money and possessions than about heaven and hell combined.

- » In the Gospels, one out of every ten verses deal with money or possessions.

- » In the Bible, there are more than 500 references to prayer and less than 500 references to faith, but there are more than 2,000 references to money and possessions.

Who owns and controls all the money in the world?

- » "For all the earth is Mine [God]" (Exodus 19:5). [Brackets are the author's.]

- » "Whatever is under the whole heaven is Mine [God]" (Job 41:11). [Brackets are the author's.]

- » "The earth is the Lord's, and all that it contains, the world, and those that dwell in it" (Psalm 24:1).

- » "The silver is Mine, and the gold is Mine, declares the Lord of hosts" (Haggai 2:8).

Who has given you all that you possess?

- » "The Lord makes poor and rich: He brings low, He also exalts" (1 Samuel 2:7).

- » "It is He [God] who changes the times and the epochs; He removes kings and establishes kings; He gives wisdom to wise men and knowledge to men of understanding" (Daniel 2:21). [Brackets are the author's.]

- » "For who regards you as superior? What do you have that you did not receive? And if you did receive it, why do you boast as if you had not received it?" (1 Corinthians 4:7).

Who has given you the ability to make wealth?

> » "But you shall remember the Lord your God, for it is He who is giving you power to make wealth, that He may confirm His covenant which He swore to your fathers, as it is this day" (Deuteronomy 8:18).

Believers are not owners, they are stewards?

> » The definition of stewardship according to *Merriam-Webster* is "the conducting, supervising, or managing of something." For Christians, it is "the use of God-given resources for the accomplishment of God-given goals."
>
> » Stewardship incorporates faithfulness and trustworthiness.
>
> » Owners have "rights" and stewards have "responsibilities."
>
> » We are not owners; we are stewards. How can you be an owner, when someone else owns you (1 Corinthians 6:19-20)?

> "Therefore, if you have not been faithful in the use of unrighteous wealth, who will entrust the true riches to you?" (Luke 16:11).

> "In this case, moreover, it is required of stewards that one be found trustworthy" (1 Corinthians 4:2).

PAPA MIKE'S ASSIGNMENT:

Look over the questions and answers one more time. Is this the way you viewed your relationship with money? If it isn't, do you think you need to change how you view money? Document what changes you need to make.

_____

_____

_____

_____

How do you think being a steward of God's money and not the owner of your own money would affect the way you spend it?

_____

_____

_____

_____

The following are three ideas, I believe, that have helped me keep money in the proper perspective, using it for God's glory and not my own selfishness. Please, do not think I always followed what I am about to tell you. But I am confident that these thoughts helped me a great deal.

1. Give willingly, cheerfully, and bountifully. 2 Corinthians 8:1-5

> » The example of the "giving" Macedonians
>> » The Macedonians were physically afflicted and financially depleted.
>> » The Romans had taken possession of all their silver and gold mines, taxed the copper and iron smelting, canceled the right to cut trees for home and shipbuilding, and fought several wars on Macedonian soil.
> » What would cause these people to respond as they did?
>> » It originated with God (8:1).
>> » It continued because they were willing to give beyond what was reasonable (8:2-4).
>> » They gave themselves to the Lord first (8:5a).
>> » They were willing to follow the Lord's will (8:5b).

> "Each one must do just as he has purposed in his heart, not grudgingly or under compulsion, for God loves a cheerful giver" (2 Corinthians 9:7).

PAPA MIKE'S LIFE:

When I lived in Houston during the '70s, I got to be friends with the number one home builder in Houston. His company is still building homes in Houston and many other cities. He was a strong believer in Jesus Christ.

One day I was asking him some questions concerning giving to the Lord, and he had three comments. Diane and I have attempted to live these out, and I can tell you because of these, I have given more than I would have ever given had he not mentioned these to me.

- » You need to plan to be a generous giver. Make it part of your monthly budget.

- » Whatever you give, visualize yourself putting it in Jesus's hands. Then you will not want to take it back when they spend money in a way you don't agree with. This has happened to me multiple times.

- » Whatever you give away, no one can take away from you. I like that the best!

PAPA MIKE'S ASSIGNMENT:

What kind of giver are you?

_____

_____

What kind of giver do you want to be?

_____

_____

What do you need to do differently to go from where you are to where you want to be?

_____

_____

2. Give sacrificially – this should be your goal.

> » Reflect on God's gifts to you. Psalm 103:1-5
> The principle: We need to count our blessings one by one and do it frequently. If we do, I believe, we will become a more generous giver.

PAPA MIKE'S ASSIGNMENT:

List at least ten blessings God has given you. After you have listed them, thank God for each one.

_____

_____

_____

_____

_____

_____

_____

_____

> » Remind yourself of God's promises regarding generosity. Proverbs 11:24, 22:9; Luke 6:38; 2 Corinthians 9:6
> The principle: We need to remember what God has said with respect to generosity.
> Please note, I am not a prosperity gospel guy. But we do serve a very generous God, and He wants us to be generous givers!

- » Reverently compare your generosity with God's. John 3:16

God	the greatest Giver
so loved	the greatest motive
the world	the greatest need
that He gave	the greatest act
His only Son	the greatest gift
that whosoever	the greatest invitation
believes in Him	the greatest opportunity
should not perish	the greatest deliverance
but have eternal life	the greatest joy

  The principle: We need to look at God's generosity when trying to determine how generous we are and should be.

- » Relate your generosity to the poor widow's. Mark 12:41-44; Luke 21:1-4
  Please notice what you can learn from Luke 21:1-4:

  - » Nothing goes unnoticed by Jesus.

  - » The rich were not condemned by their giving, but they were condemned by how they were giving— they were giving out of their surplus (vs 4)!

  - » Christ does not evaluate your giving by how much you give. He evaluates your giving by looking into your heart!

  - » How is your giving compared to this woman's giving?

  - » She gave 1/64 of a day's wage, but Christ stated she had given more than all the rest of them!

  The principle: We need to look into our hearts rather than our wallets prior to giving.

PAPA MIKE'S ASSIGNMENT:

When you give, do you always look at how much you have in your wallet or checking account before you give? I recognize you want to be wise in your giving. But maybe you need to look at the need first and then adjust what you think your wants and needs are. I know a man under 45 who has given a very large percent of his IRA two different times to his church—that's generosity!

PAPA MIKE'S AND DEE DEE'S LIVES:

Each month Diane and I had been putting aside a certain amount of money to be used as our freewill offering. It was mainly used to minister to people. When we lived in California, Diane went to visit a dear friend who did not have any extra money. Her husband was a gardener for a Christian school in the area. When Diane arrived, the lady looked concerned. Diane asked her why. She told Diane she had just gotten back from a doctor's visit for their baby. The doctor told her that her baby was cross-eyed and that if they did not have an operation very soon, their daughter's eyes would be permanently cross-eyed. The doctor told her he would not do the operation without the money upfront. They did not have the money, but Diane prayed with her. When Diane got home (this was before cell phones), she called me and told me the story. We did not have that amount in our freewill offering envelope. But we knew that God wanted us to meet this need. It was our preference to give money anonymously, but in this circumstance, that wasn't possible. Diane went to the bank and then took the money to the lady. Today that little girl is all grown up and able to see clearly because we were faithful. AMEN!

> » Relate your generosity with David's mighty men. 2 Samuel 23:13–17
> When David realized their gift could have cost his men their lives, he deemed himself unworthy of the gift. Therefore, he poured it out to the Lord, who was and is totally worthy.
> The principle: We need to realize that a gift may cost us. We need to give, releasing any ownership of how the recipient responds.
>
> » Relate your generosity with Zaccheus's. Luke 19:8–10
> Look at what we learned from Zaccheus:
>
>> » He stood; he had something to say.
>>
>> » He gave half to the poor. Nothing in the Old Testament commanded that!

» He restored four times as much to any man he had defrauded. The Old Testament taught that he should make restitution for it in full and add 20 percent more, not four times (Leviticus 6:1-7; Numbers 5:6-7).

Zaccheus did not quibble over the terms of the Law; he offered to pay a higher price because his heart had truly been changed.

What would you be willing to give in response to the eternal life Christ gave to you?
The principle: We need to realize that a changed life will yield a grateful and generous life. When was the last time you were generous?

» Remember to examine your heart. Psalm 26:2; 139:23-24
The principle: We need to evaluate our heart on an ongoing basis.

PAPA MIKE'S ASSIGNMENT:

Document any of your thoughts on this last section about giving sacrificially.

_____

_____

_____

_____

_____

3. Giving to the Lord's work. 1 Chronicles 29:1-22
   (This is one of my favorite chapters on giving in the Bible.)

   » David realized the work was for the Lord and not for man (29:1).
   Principle: When you give to your church, consider that your giving is for God's work and not just for a building or an organization or the leadership.

   » David reacted as he did because he really loved the work of the Lord (1 Chronicles 29:2-5a).
   Note: A talent is seventy-five pounds.

- » Gold - 225,000 pounds - 3,600,000 ounces at $1,776/ounce = $6,394,000,000 (in today's price of gold - 2021)

- » Silver - 525,000 pounds - 8,400,000 ounces at $26/ounce = $218,000,000 (in today's price of silver - 2021)

Principle: Our giving should be a response of love for the Lord rather than a duty.

» David requested the people to give willingly and consecrate themselves to the Lord (1 Chronicles 29:5b).
Principle: Put the Lord first in your life.

» The people rejoiced with the opportunity to say thanks to God (1 Chronicles 29:6-9).
Principle: Give to the Lord with a heart of rejoicing.

PAPA MIKE'S COMMENTS:

» Did you notice the leaders set the example (v. 6), and the people gave and rejoiced with their whole heart (v. 9)?

» Do you rejoice when the offering plate is passed?

» Do you look forward to getting to church to put your money in the offering plate?

» When was the last time you were excited about giving something to God?

» Why can't we see giving just as much a part of the worship service as the singing, the message, and the invitation?

When analyzing all the components of the worship service, your giving might represent the most sacrificial part of the service.

» David remembered what he gave already belonged to God (1 Chronicles 29:10-16).
Principle: Remember, we are only stewards and not owners. Whatever you give, you are giving what already belongs to God.

- » David recognized the importance of being right with God (1 Chronicles 29:17).
  Principle: If you see things in your life that need to be dealt with, take the time now to confess and turn from them.

- » The people returned all the glory and blessings and honor back to the Lord (1 Chronicles 29:18-20).
  Principle: Make your giving all about the Lord and not about you—don't take personal credit for your giving.

- » The people worshipped God with great gladness (1 Chronicles 29:21-22).
  Principle: When you give to God's work, it is a form of worship.

Now, let's get back to Proverbs.

Negative ways to handle money.

- » Cosigning (6:1-5; 22:26)
  - » When you cosign a loan, you and the other person complete the loan application. If the other person does not keep up with his payments, you will be required to pay the monthly payments until the loan has been paid off.
  - » A cosigner helps the borrower get approved. Without their help, the borrower would not get the loan.
  - » Even the Federal Trade Commission warns about cosigning on its website!
- » Borrowing (22:7)
- » Bribing (17:8, 23; 21:14)
- » Cheating (10:2; 11:1; 13:11; 15:27; 16:11; 20:10, 17, 23; 21:6)
- » Get rich quick schemes (20:21)
- » Robbing the poor (22:22-23)
- » Mocking the poor (17:5)
- » Oppressing the poor (14:31; 22:16)
- » Shutting their ears or eyes to the poor (21:13; 29:7)

- » Withholding good when they are able to do it (3:27-28)

- » Setting their minds on gaining wealth (23:4-5)

PAPA MIKE'S ASSIGNMENT:

Read through the eleven negative ways of handling money. Put a check mark by any that apply to you. What are some ways you can change in regard to the items you checked? What specific actions do you need to take?

_____
_____
_____
_____
_____

Positive ways of handling money:

- » Generous Giving (Proverbs 11:24-26; 14:21, 31; 19:17; 22:9)

- » Saving (Proverbs 6:6-8)

- » Giving to the Lord (Proverbs 3:9-10)

PAPA MIKE'S ASSIGNMENT:

Once again, read through these three positive ways of handling money. In which one of these do you need to do more? How do you plan to do that?

_____
_____
_____

CHAPTER 17

Principle #10 – The Value of Hard Work

Before we examine what Proverbs says about work, I would like to share a few things from the Old Testament concerning the subject.

» God and Jesus have worked from the beginning (Genesis 1:2-3, 6-7, 9, 11, 14, 16, 20-21, 24-27 ; 2:1-3; John 4:34; 5:17).

» God created man in His image as a worker, and His desire was for man to work from the beginning (Genesis 1:26-28), before the fall of man (Genesis 2:15), and after the fall (Genesis 3:17-19). It was included in the law (Exodus 20:9), the Psalms (Psalm 104:23), and in Ecclesiastes (Ecclesiastes 3:11-13; 5:18-19).

PAPA MIKE'S ASSIGNMENT:

Do you see your job—no matter if it is at home, in an office building, on an assembly line, or working out of doors—as a reward and a gift from God?

_____

_____

_____

> » In the New Testament, God desires us to work. (2 Thessalonians 3:7-15; work is mentioned in verses 8, 10, 11, 12). If we do not provide for our families, we are less than an unbeliever (1 Timothy 5:8).

PAPA MIKE'S ASSIGNMENT:

If others saw your attitude toward work, would they see God's principles being applied to your life?

_____
_____
_____
_____

Do you complain about work, or do you enjoy it? If I asked your friends or your mom and dad, what would they say?

_____
_____
_____
_____

God expects us to obey, fear, and respect our employers. The following verses are directed to slaves, but I believe can be applied to a normal worker.

> Slaves, be obedient to those who are your masters according to the flesh, with fear and trembling [right attitude], in the sincerity of your heart [right commitment], as to Christ; not by way of eyeservice, as men-pleasers, but as slaves of Christ, doing the will of God from the heart [right motivation]. With good will render service, as to the Lord, and not to men, knowing that whatever good thing each one does, this he will receive back from the Lord, whether slave or free" (Ephesians 6:5-8). [Remember: God knows, and God rewards.] [Brackets are the author's.]

PAPA MIKE'S ASSIGNMENT:

How is your attitude and commitment to your job? Are you motivated to do the best job possible?

_____

_____

_____

_____

We are also to work as if our employer is Christ (Colossians 3:23-24).

PAPA MIKE'S ASSIGNMENT:

Do you see yourself as working for Christ? Hint: When you have done all that is expected of you, ask yourself, "What is one extra thing I can do before I consider the job done?"

_____

_____

_____

_____

God desires us to work with the goal of helping others (Ephesians 4:28).

PAPA MIKE'S ASSIGNMENT:

This goes back to the previous lesson on generosity. If you are a hard worker, you have a good possibility to be able to bless others with your ability to give. Does being generous come to mind when you think of working hard or does being able to "get more stuff"?

_____

_____

God wants you to beware of "wanting too much" or "loving money" (Luke 12:15; 1 Timothy 6:10; Hebrews 13:5). Beware of coveting (Exodus 20:17; Romans 13:9).

PAPA MIKE'S ASSIGNMENT:

Check your heart honestly: How is your greed? How is your coveting?

_____

_____

_____

_____

God's desire is for us to be content (Philippians 4:11-12; 1 Timothy 6:8-9).

- » Thank God for what you have.

- » Take care of what you have.

- » Consider how much God has given you.

- » Learn to say, "No!" in regard to things you may want to buy but can't afford, don't really need, aren't your highest priority, etc. A good rule of thumb is to wait a week before making a spontaneous purchase.

Be careful that you don't fall into our culture's perspective of work.

- » The ultimate purpose of work is for you to find complete fulfillment. How is this a lie?

    This view of work expects more of work than work can ever deliver. The person who builds his self-worth on career success builds his life on a very shaky foundation. See Luke 12:13-21. What happens when things don't go well, or one day you wake up and find you are stuck and not going anywhere? If you are scratching to make it to the top, I bet you are not focusing on putting other's people's interests above your own (Philippians 2:3-4). You might also find out that one day you will be on the top, but you will be all alone.

- » Success in life means that you are successful at your work. How is this a lie?

  Many have bought into the following statement, "What we do often translates to who we are." I believe this can lead to work becoming an idol; the first commandments say a lot about that (Exodus 20:3).

- » You can tell how successful someone is by his material wealth, professional recognition, or positional status. How is this a lie?

  This view of work changes the definition of success as God has stated it. I believe at the core, God would define success as you glorifying Him (1 Corinthians 10:31), pleasing Him (Colossians 1:10), and serving Him and others (John 13:5-11; Philippians 2:3-4).

- » You have got to do whatever it takes to get the job done. How is this a lie?

  Your job is important, but it is not number one. Many a man has become a workaholic because of this philosophy! Once again, look at the first commandment (Exodus 20:3).

- » You just go to work to earn a living, and that is it. How is this a lie?

  We are Christ's ambassadors (Ephesians 6:20); therefore, we can never do anything from the perspective of just getting that activity done. We must always live out Christ's character (fruit of the Spirit) as well as bringing the gospel with us no matter where we go and who we are with. It changes your whole perspective toward work when you are aware of God's presence with you wherever you are.

Now, let's get back to Proverbs.

God blesses the person who is diligent.

- » "But the hand of the diligent makes rich" (10:4).

- » "The hand of the diligent will rule" (12:24).

- » "The precious possession of a man is diligence" (12:27).

> » "The soul of the diligent is made fat" (13:4).
>
> » "The plans of the diligent lead surely to advantage" (21:5).

> "Do you see a man skilled [you don't get to be skilled without being diligent] in his work? He will stand before kings; He will not stand before obscure men" (22:29). [Brackets are the author's.]

PAPA MIKE'S ASSIGNMENT:

Would you be considered diligent by people who know you? How do you define diligence? (It might be helpful to look up the definition.)

_____

_____

_____

_____

Consider the example God gives of the ant.

> "Go to the ant, O sluggard, observe her ways and be wise, which, having no chief, officer or ruler [I call that inner motivation], prepares her food in the summer and gathers her provision in the harvest [I call that being a hard worker and a diligent planner]" (Proverbs 6:6–8). [Brackets are the author's.]

> "How long will you lie down, O sluggard? When will you arise from your sleep? 'A little sleep, a little slumber, a little folding of the hands to rest'—your poverty will come in like a vagabond and your need like an armed man" (Proverbs 6:9-11). (I call this the downward spiral of becoming a sluggard.)
>
> » Be self-motivated.
>
> » Be a tireless worker.
>
> » Plan for the future.
>
> » Recognize slothfulness and avoid it!

PAPA MIKE'S ASSIGNMENT:

Which verses characterize your work ethic (Proverbs 6:6-8 or Proverbs 6:9-11)? Why did you choose that answer?

_____

_____

_____

_____

God wants us to reject the silent killer of being a slothful man.

A slothful man:

- » Does not see how unwise he really is (26:16)
- » Does not see that making soft choices in life is deadly (6:10-11; 12:24; 19:15, 20:4)
- » Does not finish his tasks (12:27; 24:30-31)
- » Desires or dreams more than he does work, therefore nothing is accomplished (21:25-26)
- » Indulges himself [e.g., with food (19:24) and sleep (26:14)] and therefore does not accomplish the tasks that are before him
- » Hurts his employer (10:26)
- » Is a victim of self-induced fears (22:13)

PAPA MIKE'S ASSIGNMENT:

Review this list again. Is there an area in which you need to repent? Once you have identified your issue, develop steps to correct your issues. Being slothful is deadly.

_____

_____

_____

_____

If you see slothfulness as an area you need to work on, consider God's solution:

> "For even when we were with you, we used to give you this order: if anyone is not willing to work, then he is not to eat, either" (2 Thessalonians 3:10).

Perhaps to remind yourself that work is important, you could fast one day a week until you see your attitude changing.

PAPA MIKE'S LIFE:

I have always enjoyed work. I'm not sure why, but maybe it was because my dad made me work with him when I was a small boy. Also, I grew up in a family that valued work. If there was something to do, we all got involved. No one just sat around. We all had to join in to finish the task.

One attitude that really helped me during my years at Union Carbide, FamilyLife, and BCLR was being a servant, even when I was a manager. Wanting to help people who reported to me, I believe, made me a better leader. It seems that all my jobs, no matter what they were, had a component of "helping someone."

As a purchasing manager in Union Carbide, my department had the responsibility of purchasing many different items for many different people or departments. But one thing was common. Each of those requisitioners were asking us to purchase something they needed. We could lord over them by substituting a different item or denying their request, or we could work hard to understand what they needed and serve them while following all the purchasing policies and procedures of Union Carbide. I believe the last perspective is the more biblical approach.

> "But Jesus called them to Himself and said, 'You know that the rulers of the Gentiles lord it over them, and their great men exercise authority over them. It is not this way among you, but whoever wishes to become great among you shall be your servant, and whoever wishes to be first among you shall be your slave; just as the Son of Man did not come to be served, but to serve, and to give His life a ransom for many.'" (Matthew 20:25-28). (See also Mark 10:42-45 and Luke 22:24-27.)

I remember when I was a purchasing manager in Charleston, West Virginia, that one of my employees was blind and had a seeing eye dog. When I took over as purchasing manager, this person was already there. One day, his dog vomited, and it smelled horrible! No one would clean it up. Someone called the department responsible for cleaning, but they were going to be a while, and the smell was bad. I went into the janitor's closet, got everything I needed, and proceeded to clean up the mess. While doing it, I thought about John 13 and Jesus washing the disciple's feet. Sometimes you only get one chance to wash someone's feet. Be available! Needless to say, my employees were blown away that I would clean up the mess.

CHAPTER 18

Principle # 11 – Control Your Anger

Anger has its proper time, place, issue, and portion, and that is called righteous anger. But you need to be very wise because I would say 95 percent of anger does not fall into that category.

> We are told that we can be angry and not sin: "Be angry, and yet do not sin; do not let the sun go down on your anger" (Ephesians 4:26).

Jesus was angered due to others' hardness of heart.

> "He [Jesus] entered again into a synagogue; and a man was there whose hand was withered. They were watching Him to see if He would heal him on the Sabbath, so that they might accuse Him. He said to the man with the withered hand, 'Get up and come forward!' And He said to them, 'Is it lawful to do good or to do harm on the Sabbath, to save a life or to kill?' But they kept silent. After looking around at them with anger, grieved at their hardness of heart, He said to the man, 'Stretch out your hand.' And he stretched it out, and his hand was restored" (Mark 3:1–5). [Brackets are the author's.]

God was angered due to various reasons:

- After the death of Joshua, Israel followed other gods (Judges 2:8-12).

- God told the Israelites in Numbers 4:15 that no one could touch the ark of God. Uzzah didn't obey and was irreverent (2 Samuel 6:6-7).
    - The wickedness, evil, and sins of the kings of Israel provoked God to anger.
    - Jeroboam (1 Kings 15:30)
    - Baasha (1 Kings 15:27, 16:1-3)
    - Omri (1 Kings 16:25-26)
    - Ahab (1 Kings 16:29-33; 21:20-22)
    - Ahaziah (1 Kings 22:51-53)
    - Manasseh (2 Kings 21:1-6)

How you need to live in the light of anger:

- It is a beautiful thing to be self-controlled (16:32; 19:11).
- It is wise to keep away from a man given to anger (22:24-25).
- A wise man will turn away anger (29:8).
- The person who is slow to anger has great understanding (14:29).
- If you want to calm a situation, respond with a gentle answer (15:1) and be slow to anger (15:18).

How you don't want to live in the light of anger:

- Living with a contentious (critical spirit or faultfinding) woman is not easy (21:9; 25:24; 27:15).
- If you don't control your spirit, you will be wide open to all kinds of trouble (25:28).
- An angry man stirs up strife (29:22, 30:33).
- A man of great anger will suffer penalties (19:19).
- Anger is like a flood, and it will cause much devastation (27:4).
- Anger and a fool go hand in hand (29:11).

Our country is losing the battle with anger.

- » Road rage
- » Political rage
- » Domestic violence
- » Child abuse

Spiritual side of anger

> "Now the deeds of the flesh are evident, which are: immorality, impurity, sensuality, idolatry, sorcery, enmities, strife, jealousy, outbursts of anger, disputes, dissensions, factions, envying, drunkenness, carousing, and things like these, of which I forewarn you, just as I have forewarned you, that those who practice such things will not inherit the kingdom of God" (Galatians 5:19-21).

PAPA MIKE'S ASSIGNMENT:

If you are a person given to anger, take time to read *The Heart of Anger* by Lou Priolo[1] (focus on chapters 6-8).

Please take notes:

_____
_____
_____
_____
_____
_____
_____

---

[1] Lou Priolo. *The Heart of Anger.* Calvary Press Publishing, 1997.

CHAPTER 19

Principle #12 – Be a Good Listener and a God Honoring Speaker

Seven benefits to listening

- » It gives you time to understand.
- » It gives you freedom to observe.
- » It allows you time to think.
- » It provides you space to feel.
- » It broadens your awareness.
- » It communicates care and concern.
- » It gives you knowledge on how to pray.

Types of listeners that you should not be:

- » "Half ear"
- » "Even though I'm talking to the other person, I am still listening."

- » "Even though I am on the phone, I am still listening."
- » "I can interpret two conversations at once."
- » "Don't let the fact that I am reading a book keep you from talking".
- » "Walk in and out of the room while you are talking."
- » "I am going to just rest my eyes a bit."
- » "I can do at least three other things while you are talking."
- » "Interrupt constantly."
- » "I will listen for thirty seconds."
- » "I will formulate my answer while you are talking."

Seven things you should incorporate into your listening:

- » Look into their eyes—that will help more than anything.
- » Engage in the conversation and inquire by saying, "Please, tell me more."
- » Stop interrupting with your "answers."
- » Tell them what you heard them say and ask them if you understood correctly.
- » Never look at your watch or phone while they are talking.
- » Listen with everything you have. It requires energy, focus, and endurance. Be careful with your gestures, facial expressions, tone of voice, folding your arms, rolling your eyes, shaking your head, sighing deeply, or walking toward the door.
- » Listen with an open mind—pride will keep you deaf.

You must listen to understand each other.

- » It will take work (2:2; 4:1; 5:1).
- » It is available (8:1).
- » It is from the Lord (2:5-6; 28:5).

- » God tells us to acquire it (4:5, 7).
- » Understanding is valuable (16:16, 22).
- » "He who keeps understanding will find good" (19:8).
- » Homes are established by understanding (24:3).
- » Understanding leads to long life (28:2).
- » Blessed is the man who finds wisdom and gains understanding (3:13–16).

PAPA MIKE'S ASSIGNMENT:

Go over all the above notes. Please identify two things you need to quit doing and two things you need to start doing.

Things you need to quit doing:

_____

_____

_____

_____

Things you need to start doing:

_____

_____

_____

_____

How are your words powerful?

> "The one who guards his mouth preserves his life; the one who opens wide his lips comes to ruin" (13:3).

> "A man has joy in an apt answer, and how delightful is a timely word!" (15:23).

> "Righteous lips are the delight of kings, and he who speaks right is loved" (16:13).

> "Death and life are in the power of the tongue" (18:21).

> "Whoever guards his mouth and tongue, guards his soul from troubles." (21:23).

> "And my inmost being will rejoice when your lips speak what is right" (23:16).

What should be the goal of your talk?

> "All the utterances of my mouth are in righteousness; there is nothing crooked or perverted in them" (8:8).

With respect to your talk, what does God hate, and what is an abomination to Him (6:16-17, 19; 12:22)?

What should you do if you "talk wrong" (6:2-5)?

You should choose your words carefully. Each one of these verses are a contrast between your words being a blessing or a curse.

> "The mouth of the righteous is a fountain of life, but the mouth of the wicked conceals violence" (10:11).

> "Wise men store up knowledge, but with the mouth of the foolish, ruin is at hand" (10:14).

> "He who despises his neighbor lacks sense, but a man of understanding keeps silent" (11:12).

> "An evil man is ensnared by the transgression of his lips, but the righteous will escape from trouble" (12:13).

> "Lying lips are an abomination to the Lord, but those who deal faithfully are His delight" (12:22).

> "Anxiety in a man's heart weighs him down, but a good word makes him glad" (12:25).

> "From the fruit of a man's mouth he enjoys good, but the desire of the treacherous is violence" (13:2).

> "A righteous man hates falsehood, but a wicked man acts disgustingly and shamefully" (13:5).

> "A trustworthy witness will not lie, but a false witness utters lies" (14:5).

> "A truthful witness saves lives, but he who utters lies is treacherous" (14:25).

> "The mind of the intelligent seeks knowledge, but the mouth of fools feeds on folly" (15:14).

> "The heart of the righteous ponders how to answer, but the mouth of the wicked pours out evil things" (15:28).

> "The poor man utters supplications, but the rich man answers roughly" (18:23).

> "Keeping away from strife is an honor for a man, but any fool will quarrel" (20:3).

> "Bread obtained by falsehood is sweet to a man, but afterward his mouth will be filled with gravel" (20:17).

PAPA MIKE'S ASSIGNMENT:

In light of these sections, list the things you learned about words that you did not know before you read these Proverbs.

_____

_____

_____

_____

What are some warnings concerning the tongue?

- » Slander (making a false statement damaging another person's reputation) (10:18; 16:28; 20:19)

- » Dishonesty and lying (See "good name and integrity" in chapter 23.)

- » Foolish speech (18:6–7)

- » Scoffer (one who laughs or speaks about someone in a way that shows they think the person is stupid or silly) (15:12, 22:10)

- » Hasty, impulsive, rash speech (10:19, 18:13, 29:20)

- » Quarreling, harsh words (19:19; 25:24; 26:21; 27:15; 29:20)

- » Perverse speech (opposing what is right, reasonable, or accepted) (6:12)

- » Gossip (17:9; 18:8; 20:19; 26:22)

- » Speaking without thinking (13:3; 18:13; 29:20)

- » Telling secrets (11:13)

PAPA MIKE'S ASSIGNMENT:

Considering the warnings above. From which one of these do you need to confess? Find a way to hold yourself accountable from not doing that particular speech any longer. You can keep a card and make a mark on it each time you say it or wear a stretchy wristband and transfer it to the other wrist whenever you slip up. We know a couple who paid each other a certain amount each time they said something negative!

_____

_____

_____

_____

What are the positive aspects of talking biblically?

What are the mouth, lips, or words compared to in the book of Proverbs?

- » "The tongue of the righteous is as choice silver" (10:20).

- » "A soothing tongue is a tree of life" (15:4).

- » "Pleasant words are a honeycomb, sweet to the soul and healing to the bones" (16:24).

- » "There is gold, and an abundance of jewels; but the lips of knowledge are a more precious thing" (20:15).

- » "Like apples of gold in settings of silver is a word spoken in right circumstances" (25:11).

By what should our talk be characterized, and what are the benefits of righteous talk?

- » "But he who restrains his lips is wise" (10:19).

- » "The mouth of the righteous flows with wisdom" (10:31).

- » "The lips of the righteous bring forth what is acceptable" (10:32).

- » "But the mouth of the upright will deliver them" (12:6).

- » "But the tongue of the wise brings healing" (12:18).

- » "But a good word makes it [the heart] glad" (12:25). [Brackets are the author's.]

- » "The one who guards his mouth preserves his life" (13:3).

- » "But the lips of the wise will protect them" (14:3).

- » "A man has joy in an apt answer, and how delightful is a timely word!" (15:23).

- » "Righteous lips are the delight of kings, and he who speaks right is loved" (16:13).

PAPA MIKE'S ASSIGNMENT:

List three to five qualities of speech that God promotes. Of the ones you listed, which ones do you need to live out more? Ask the Lord to help you incorporate them into your daily communication.

_____

_____

_____

_____

_____

_____

_____

CHAPTER 20

Principle #13 – The Right View of Sex

Singular devotion:

> "Drink water from your own cistern and fresh water from your own well. Should your springs be dispersed abroad, streams of water in the streets? Let them be yours alone and not for strangers with you" (Proverbs 5:15-17).

Satisfied devotion:

> "Let your fountain be blessed, and rejoice in the wife of your youth. As a loving hind and a graceful doe, let her breasts satisfy you at all times; be exhilarated always with her love" (Proverbs 5:18-19).

PAPA MIKE'S COMMENTS:

Please, please, please, I know the culture is saying, "Just do it." They say it's not a big deal, but God says otherwise; therefore, who do you want to believe, the world or God? I hope and pray you pick God.

> "Flee immorality. Every other sin that a man commits is outside the body, but the immoral man sins against his own body" (1 Corinthians 6:18).

> Now flee from youthful lusts and pursue righteousness, faith, love and peace, with those who call on the Lord from a pure heart" (2 Timothy 2:22).

IMPORTANT: Can I say one more thing to anyone who is involved in pornography? Please read Heath Lambert's book, *Finally Free*[2], and see things that will affect your life for a very long time.

---

[2] Heath Lambert. *Finally Free: Fighting for Purity with the Power of Grace.* Zondervan, 2013.

CHAPTER 21

Principle #14 – Daughters, Be an Excellent Wife

The value of an excellent wife.

> "An excellent wife, who can find? For her worth is far above jewels" (Proverbs 31:10).

> "An excellent wife is the crown of her husband, but she who shames him is like rottenness in his bones" (Proverbs 12:4).

> "House and wealth are an inheritance from fathers, but a prudent wife is from the Lord" (Proverbs 19:14).

Be trusted by your husband.

> "The heart of her husband trusts in her, and he will have no lack of gain" (Proverbs 31:11).

Be a helpmate to your husband every day.

> "She does him good and not evil all the days of her life" (Proverbs 31:12).

Be industrious.

> "She looks for wool and flax and works with her hands in delight. She is like merchant ships; she brings her food from afar" (Proverbs 31:13-14).

Don't be slothful.

> "She rises also while it is still night" (Proverbs 31:15a).

Be generous.

> "And gives food to her household and portions to her maidens" (Proverbs 31:15b).

> "She extends her hand to the poor, and she stretches out her hands to the needy" (Proverbs 31:20).

Handle money well.

> "She considers a field and buys it; from her earnings she plants a vineyard" (Proverbs 31:16).

Be a hard worker.

> "She girds herself with strength and makes her arms strong. She senses that her gain is good; her lamp does not go out at night. She stretches out her hands to the distaff, and her hands grasp the spindle" (Proverbs 31:17–19).

> "She is not afraid of the snow for her household, for all her household are clothed with scarlet. She makes coverings for herself; her clothing is fine linen and purple" (Proverbs 31:21–22).

> "She makes linen garments and sells them, and supplies belts to the tradesmen" (Proverbs 31:24).

> "She looks well to the ways of her household, and does not eat the bread of idleness" (Proverbs 31:27).

Desire for your husband to be all that God would have him to be.

> "Her husband is known in the gates, when he sits among the elders of the land" (Proverbs 31:23).

Be a woman of character and one who smiles at the future.

> "Strength and dignity are her clothing, and she smiles at the future" (Proverbs 31:25).

Have wisdom and kindness foremost in your mind.

> "She opens her mouth in wisdom, and the teaching of kindness is on her tongue" (Proverbs 31:26).

Recognize the benefits of this type of life.

> "Her children rise up and bless her; her husband also, and he praises her, saying: 'Many daughters have done nobly, but you excel them all'" (Proverbs 31:28-29).

> "Give her the product of her hands, and let her works praise her in the gates" (Proverbs 31:31).

Have a life that fears the Lord.

> "Charm is deceitful, and beauty is vain, but a woman who fears the Lord, she shall be praised" (Proverbs 31:30).

PAPA MIKE'S COMMENTS:

Ladies: To do all the things listed in Proverbs 31 is an overwhelming goal! But one thing is clear: A godly woman is not bored, dull, or unchallenged in life. This chapter paints a picture of a woman who is reaching her full potential while she cares for others. It is the opposite of the way the world portrays a woman who works in her home or out of her home.

This woman is honest, industrious, energetic, creative, resourceful, compassionate, submissive to her husband, strong and fit, knowledgeable, and God honoring. And she does all these things while maintaining her individuality.

I'm sure if you studied this chapter in depth, you could find more, but my suggestion for you is to seek to improve in one or two of these qualities whether you are married or not.

Men: Look for godly women to date, not the best looking or most popular.

PAPA MIKE'S PRAYER

Ladies, I truly pray that you will take these verses to heart. Amen!

CHAPTER 22

Principle # 15 – Embrace Humility and Reject Pride

"There are six things which the Lord hates, yes, seven which are an abomination to Him: haughty eyes, a lying tongue, and hands that shed innocent blood" (6:16-17).

"When pride comes, then comes dishonor, but with the humble is wisdom" (11:2).

"Through insolence [pride] comes nothing but strife" (13:10). [Brackets are the author's]

"The Lord will tear down the house of the proud" (15:25).

"And before honor comes humility" (15:33).

"Everyone who is proud in heart is an abomination to the Lord" (16:5).

"Pride goes before destruction, and a haughty spirit before stumbling" (16:18).

"The reward of humility and the fear of the Lord are riches, honor and life" (22:4b).

"A man's pride will bring him low, but a humble spirit will obtain honor" (29:23).

PAPA MIKE'S COMMENTS:

Did you notice how much more is said to the proud than to the humble?

- » The Lord hates haughty eyes.
- » The Lord hates pride and arrogance.
- » Pride and dishonor and destruction and stumbling go together.
- » Insolence brings strife.
- » The proud will have their house torn down.
- » The proud are an abomination to the Lord.
- » The proud will be brought low.

Isn't that enough for you to want to kill pride in your life?

If you are serious about killing pride and cultivating humility, work through Stewart Scott's book, *Pride to Humility*.[3] It will change your life, I promise. It has changed mine, and I have worked through this book four or five times. Every time I worked through it, I was again confronted with my pride and lack of humility in specific areas.

An additional comment:

I've worked with many men who realize life is not going well for them, but they didn't realize that they had a problem with pride. Ask people you trust to honestly tell you if this is a blind spot in your life.

---

3   Stuart Scott. *Pride to Humility*. Focus Publishing, 2003.

CHAPTER 23

Principle # 16 – The Value of a Good Name and Integrity

Good name:

> "The memory of the righteous is blessed, but the name of the wicked will rot" (Proverbs 10:7).

> "A good name is to be more desired than great" (Proverbs 22:1a).

> "A good name is better than a good ointment, and the day of one's death is better than the day of one's birth" (Ecclesiastes 7:1).

PAPA MIKE'S LIFE:

While Diane and I were living in West Virginia, I got a refund check from the IRS for $3,000. The very next day, I dropped it off in the night depository at our bank (yes, this was back in the dark ages; the internet was not yet discovered). At the end of the month, I got my statement from the bank, but it did not reflect my deposit from the IRS. I called the bank and talked to the accounting manager. She told me she would investigate it. A couple of days later, she called me and told me that no check for $3,000 was deposited in any account during that entire week.

I then learned the process for getting a replacement check from the IRS—OUCH—what a mess! It was a busy time in my life, and I just did not get to it. Three months passed. While I was at work, I got a call from the accounting manager; she told me they found the check. It had been deposited in the wrong account. She was extremely apologetic. I responded with a big "Praise the Lord!" and told her that I had not yet submitted the forms to the IRS to get a replacement check. She again apologized for not seeing it the first time. I told her, "No big deal. Just deposit it. Life is great!" Then there was a pause on the phone, and she asked if I knew her. I told her that her name did not ring a bell, but if I had met her, please forgive me. She then told me she had visited my Sunday school class over a year ago. She said the way I responded to this situation was not typical. She expected to be yelled at, so my response surprised her. She then stated that I truly lived out my faith. You never know who you are talking to, and you only have one chance to keep your good name and be a person of integrity.

Integrity and being a person of conviction—you should know what you believe and live for those beliefs.

- "He is a shield to those who walk in integrity" (2:7b).

- "He who walks in integrity walks securely" (10:9a).

- "The integrity of the upright will guide them" (11:3a).

- "A righteous man who walks in his integrity—how blessed are his sons after him" (20:7).

PAPA MIKE'S LIFE:

When I was joining FamilyLife, two things happened that tested my convictions. These concerned what I believe about the Word of God versus what would be the expedient thing to do. I believe every word of God is from Him and is true. I might have a problem understanding it, but it is true no matter what.

FamilyLife wanted people to know for certain that God was "calling" them to this ministry. I was at lunch with a recruiter and his wife, and she asked me about my "call." I told her I was very confident about coming to FamilyLife, but I could not tell her that I was totally confident that this was God's call for Diane and me. I then clarified that the only thing I could be totally confident about was what was written in God's Word. That was not what she wanted to hear. She questioned me again, but I gave her the same answer. Her husband finally stopped the conversation and told me that my position was fine.

A few days later, I was filling out the final application, and I came to a question that asked, "Are you committed to stay with FamilyLife for a minimum of four years?" I called a vice president of human resources and told him I could not guarantee that I would stay at FamilyLife for four years because I was still hoping to get a church administrator's job; if one materialized before four years, I would leave FamilyLife. I also told him if something else happened in my life, and I knew God was leading me away from FamilyLife, I would leave FamilyLife. He tried to convince me to sign the document anyway, but I would not. He told me he would have to get approval and that it might not happen. I told him if they would not approve me unless I signed the document, then I would take that as a word from the Lord that it was not His intention for me to join FamilyLife. He called back in a couple of hours and told me to skip that question.

Now, for the for the rest of the story. I joined FamilyLife October 31, 2002. I was hired to be the church administrator of The Bible Church of Little Rock on January 12, 2007. Four years and two and a half months later. God is good!

CHAPTER 24

Principle #17 – Be Honest and Avoid Lying at All Costs

"Put away from you a deceitful mouth" (4:24a).

"There are six things which the Lord hates, yes, seven which are an abomination to Him: . . . A false witness who utters lies" (6:16, 19).

"Truthful lips endure forever, but a lying tongue is but for a moment" (12:19 ESV).

"Lying lips are an abomination to the Lord, but those who deal faithfully are His delight" (12:22).

"A truthful witness saves lives, but he who utters lies is treacherous." (14:25).

"A dishonest man spreads strife" (16:28a ESV).

"A man of crooked heart does not discover good, and one with a dishonest tongue falls into calamity" (17:20 ESV).

> "A false witness will not go unpunished, and he who tells lies will not escape [perish]" (19:5, 9). [Brackets are the author's]

> "It is better to be a poor man than a liar" (19:22b).

> "Differing weights are an abomination to the Lord, and a false scale is not good" (20:23).

> "The getting of treasures by a lying tongue is a fleeting vapor and a snare of death" (21:6 ESV).

> "A false witness will perish, but the word of a man who hears will endure" (21:28 ESV).

> "A lying tongue hates its victims, and a flattering mouth works ruin" (26:28 ESV).

PAPA MIKE'S LIFE:

Several years ago, a man asked me if I had done something that I said that I would do. Instead of telling the truth, I told him a lie because I was embarrassed. As soon as I did it, I was convicted. The next day was Sunday. I looked for him at church, and when I found him, I went straight to him and asked him if he had a minute. He said he did, and I told him I had no excuse, but I had lied to him. I then told him the truth and why I lied. He was very disappointed in me. I asked him to forgive me, and he did.

Now for the rest of the story. This man and I became good friends. Many times, he called me for advice concerning various relationship problems he was having. In November of 2019, we left BCLR, where we had been members for seventeen years. I called this man to tell him we were leaving, and he told me he was very sad. He then related the incident of me lying to him. He told me that because I was honest about the lie, it gave him the confidence to call and ask me for wisdom concerning how he should deal with all those relationships.

PAPA MIKE'S ASSIGNMENT:

A good name and conscience are more valuable than gold! Pray and ask God to show you if there is hidden sin in your life. If there is, do everything in your power to make it right.

Diane was convicted about a prank she played on a friend long before she was a Christian. She spent time to hunt down her friend's phone number to confess and make it right. She spoke to her friend just days before the woman died of cancer. Obedience is HARD, and it's humbling, but the rewards are great!

CHAPTER 25

Principle #18 – Be a Good Friend

The benefits of having a "true" friend.

> "A friend loves at all times, and a brother is born for adversity" (17:17).

> "A man of too many friends comes to ruin, but there is a friend who sticks closer than a brother" (18:24).

> "Faithful are the wounds of a friend, but deceitful are the kisses of an enemy" (27:6).

> "Oil and perfume make the heart glad, so a man's counsel is sweet to his friend" (27:9).

Be careful with "so-called" friends.

> "Wealth adds many friends, but a poor man is separated from his friend" (19:4).

> "Many will seek the favor of a generous man, and every man is a friend to him who gives gifts" (19:6).

> "He who loves purity of heart and whose speech is gracious, the king is his friend" (22:11).

Be faithful to yours and your parent's friends.

> "Do not forsake your own friend or your father's friend" (27:10a).

PAPA MIKE'S COMMENTS:

I would like you to see in Scripture a beautiful picture of a "true friend." I am talking about the friendship between Jonathan and David.

1. A willingness to love another person as yourself (1 Samuel 18:1–2).

   God knew that David needed Jonathan far more than Jonathan needed David.

   - Sometimes friendships are for you, sometimes for the other person, and sometimes for both. But no matter what the case, everyone benefits from friendships. Be open to the friendships God wants to bring into your life.

   - Maybe the question needs to be, will you let God choose your friends like Jonathan did?

   - Don't forget what happened prior to this chapter. David had just killed "the giant." David was getting all the attention, Jonathan none. Jonathan was heir to the throne, and David was a shepherd. David could not give Jonathan anything, but Jonathan had much to give to David.

   - Are you willing to love like Jonathan?

2. A willingness to commit and covenant (1 Samuel 18:3).

   - There was a by-product of that love: Jonathan reached out to David and made a covenant with him. A covenant is like a lifelong contract, a binding promise.

   - Do you have any friends like that? If you do, you are blessed.

   - Are you willing to commit to a friendship, or are you always standing on the sidelines?

3. A willingness to give of your cherished possessions (1 Samuel 18:4).

    » Instead of shepherd clothes, Jonathan gave David royal apparel, not from his closet but from his own back.

    » Instead of shepherd's weapons, which was a rod and sling, David received a warrior's weapons.

    » These were highly valued gifts for this time.

    » Are you willing to give sacrificially to your friend?

4. A willingness to not be envious or jealous (1 Samuel 18:5-16).

    » Once again, there is not a word concerning jealousy on Jonathan's part.

    » Are you willing to not be envious or jealous of a friend's abilities and gifts, even rejoice in their successes when they possibly diminish your own?

    » Are you willing to desire the best for your friend and pray accordingly, even if it means that they might receive something you desire?

5. A willingness to be loyal for a lifetime (1 Samuel 19:1-7, 20:1-40).

    » Are you willing to be loyal even if it means risking another relationship, e.g. relatives, other friends, etc.?

    » Do you see your friendships as timeless? The sacrifices of friendship go both ways. Jonathan knows God will bless David, and now he's asking David to watch out for him in the future and stay true to their friendship.

6. A willingness to be vulnerable towards the other person (1 Samuel 20:41).

    » Are you willing to be vulnerable?

7. A willingness to remind the other person that God has brought you together, and the Lord will keep you together (1 Samuel 20:42).

    » Are you willing to remember that the Lord is the one who has brought you together, and it is the Lord who will keep you close? God brings people in and out of our lives. These men knew they might never see each other again.

8. A willingness to risk everything to encourage the other one in the Lord
(1 Samuel 23:15-17).

> Once again, Saul took his army and went after David.

> » Are you willing to do whatever is necessary to be an encouragement to your friend in the Lord?

> » A few months ago, I got a call from Paul Deakin telling us they had just moved north of Columbus, Ohio. Paul was one of my dearest friends in Charleston, West Virginia. I left Charleston in 1994. Since that conversation, I have been to his home, and he has been to my home. What a blessing!

9. A willingness to depart and go the way the Lord has directed (1 Samuel 23:18).

10. Conclusion: The results of having a friend like Jonathan (1 Samuel 30:6).

> "Moreover David was greatly distressed because the people spoke of stoning him, for all the people were embittered, each one because of his sons and his daughters. But David strengthened himself in the Lord his God" (1 Samuel 30:6).

> » Friends can be a strong influence on each other in our growth toward Christ-likeness!

PAPA MIKE'S COMMENTS:

I have dealt with lots of men over the years and have come to recognize that most of them need to do the following six things:

1. Commit to being a biblical friend like Jonathan and David.

2. Find men who will give them biblical counsel (see chapter 10).

3. Seek out spiritual men who will confront, challenge, and spur them on to godly living when they go astray or get lazy about the things of God (Proverbs 27:17).

4. Offer encouragement when their friend gets discouraged or overwhelmed (1 Samuel 23:15-17).

5. Bear each another's burdens (Galatians 6:1-2).

6. And finally, the most important—but the hardest—is to pray for one another that:

> We will be bold about sharing the message of Christ (Romans 1:16).

> We will put on the full armor of God and resist the devil (Ephesians 6:11).

> We will abound more and more in our love for one another (1 Thessalonians 3:12).

> We will approve the things that are excellent (Philippians 1:9-10).

> We will be filled with the righteousness of Christ and His will (Philippians 1:11).

> We will walk worthy of the Lord and please Him in everything we do (Colossians 1:9-10).

> We will give thanks to God in all things (1 Thessalonians 5:1).

> We will consider others more important than ourselves (Philippians 2:3-4).

> We will set our affections on things above, and fix our eyes on Jesus (Hebrews 12:1-2).

> We will live in a way that glorifies the name of God (2 Thessalonians 1:11-12).

> If married, we will love our spouses as Christ loved the church (Ephesians 5:25).

> If we have children, we will raise them up in the nurture and admonition of the Lord (Philippians 6:4).

PAPA MIKE'S PRAYER:

God, put a burden on the heart of everyone who is doing this Bible study to be a "biblical friend." Amen.

CHAPTER 26

Principle #19 – Trust God

> "Trust in the LORD with all your heart and do not lean on your own understanding. In all your ways acknowledge Him, and He will make your paths straight. Do not be wise in your own eyes; fear the LORD and turn away from evil" (Proverbs 3:5-7).

PAPA MIKE'S LIFE:

I would like to talk about how to handle disappointments in life, because they will come.

I started my career with Union Carbide at Texas City, Texas, in 1975 as an industrial engineer working for four Gulf Coast chemical plant materials management organizations. In 1978, I became a purchasing agent. In 1979, I was transferred as the materials manager of the Torrance, California, chemical plant. Two years later, I was transferred to Charleston, West Virginia, as one of the regional purchasing managers. By this time, Diane and I wanted to go back south to be closer to our families. A job became available near Houston, Texas. I applied for the job. One of my friends was offered the job, but he turned it down because he was from Michigan and did not want to move that far away from his family. Then someone else was offered the job, and they accepted it. Diane and I were very disappointed. That is when I had to start thinking through what I had learned from the Bible.

I had to believe that if God wanted me to have that job in Texas, it would have been mine.

> "It is He who changes the times and the epochs; He removes kings and establishes kings; He gives wisdom to wise men and knowledge to men of understanding" (Daniel 2:21).

I had to trust in the Lord and not lean on our understanding.

> "Trust in the Lord with all your heart and do not lean on your own understanding. In all your ways acknowledge Him, and He will make your paths straight" (Proverbs 3:5-6).

I had to recognize that this was for my good, even though it went against what I wanted.

> "And we know that God causes all things to work together for good to those who love God, to those who are called according to His purpose. For those whom He foreknew, He also predestined to become conformed to the image of His Son, so that He would be the firstborn among many brethren" (Romans 8:28-29).

I had to believe the answer for not being disappointed was to trust in God.

> "In You they trusted and were not disappointed" (Psalm 22:5b).

The story of Joseph:

- » He was sold into slavery by his brothers. (Genesis 37:25-28).

- » Potiphar's wife lied about Joseph and what he had done, and he was sent to prison. (Genesis 39:6b-23).

- » Joseph interpreted the cup bearer's and the baker's dream. Joseph's only request to the chief cupbearer was for him to remember Joseph to Pharaoh, but he didn't (Genesis 40:9-23).

- » Finally, Joseph did get to interpret a dream of Pharaoh. With that everything changed, and he became second only to Pharaoh in all of Egypt (Genesis 41:1-49).

- » Joseph saved his brothers and all their family from starvation and in the end, he stated the following: "As for you, you meant evil against me, but God meant it for good in order to bring about this present result, to preserve many people alive" (Genesis 50:20).

PAPA MIKE'S COMMENTS:

When our circumstances aren't going the way we think is best, we have to trust that God sees the whole picture and is moving us towards a higher purpose.

Please go back and read the first part of my story (pages 60-61).

It was now the spring of 2002. We had a great de-icing season. My last day at Dow Chemical was scheduled to be May 31. I finally said yes to FamilyLife and told my management at Dow that I would be retiring from Union Carbide on May 31, 2002.

This was one of the times where the pros (looking for a corporate job) outnumber the cons (becoming a missionary with FamilyLife) by a huge number. But in the end, I chose to become a missionary.

In early May, I was conducting my last meeting with all the appropriate managers of Dow Chemical. At the end of that day, I was flying to Daytona Beach, Florida, for my training with Campus Crusade for Christ (now called CRU). I arrived early to make sure everything was ready for my meeting, and my boss walked in and asked if we could visit. He told me that Dow wanted me to stay on as an employee of Dow Chemical. He stated that everyone who worked with me was very impressed with my expertise, experience, work ethic, and knowledge of the deicing business. I told him that afternoon I was heading to Daytona Beach for CRU training. He said he knew that, but Dow still wanted me to cancel my plans and become an employee of Dow. I told him it was way too late for that. He then asked me to stay on for another year. I chuckled and told him that was also impossible. Then he asked if I would stay on for six months. Still no. Finally he asked what I would do. I thought about it and told him I would stay till the end of July, which I did.

In the next six months, I raised the support I needed and reported to FamilyLife on October 31, 2002. It was a gift from the Lord to have an income while I devoted time to raising support. Diane and I joined Bible Church of Little Rock in December of 2002.

Now, fast forward to 2006. In January of 2006, I became an elder at BCLR. In November of that year, I was standing in line with our pastor at an elder's Thanksgiving dinner, and he told me that our part-time accountant was stepping down because he was taking a full-time job. He added that the deacons were considering whether it was time to hire a full-time church administrator. The next day, I contacted the chairman of the deacons and told him if they were going to hire someone, I would love to be considered. He told me they probably would not hire anyone until the end of 2007 (a year from then). I told him that was fine because I was still at FamilyLife, and I wasn't looking to change jobs. Two weeks later, he called and asked, if they were to move up the timetable to the middle of the year, would I still be interested? I told him I would.

Right around Christmas he called me again and asked, "If we were to hire someone at the first of the year would I be interested?" I told him I would. I also told him I was flying to Senegal on January 15 for three weeks to visit my son and his family. I had several meetings between January 1 and 15. But before I left for Senegal, I was offered the church administrator's job, and I accepted. On February 27, 2007, I walked into the offices of BCLR as their church administrator, the job I had wanted for years.

God is faithful, but He is faithful on His timetable and not ours. (At least I didn't have to wait forty years like Moses!)

> "Do not fret because of evildoers, be not envious toward wrongdoers. For they will wither quickly like the grass and fade like the green herb. Trust in the Lord and do good; dwell in the land and cultivate faithfulness. Delight yourself in the Lord; and He will give you the desires of your heart. Commit your way to the Lord, trust also in Him, and He will do it. He will bring forth your righteousness as the light and your judgment as the noonday. Rest in the Lord and wait patiently for Him; do not fret because of him who prospers in his way, because of the man who carries out wicked schemes" (Psalm 37:1-7).

Remember, in the late '80s, I wanted to be a church administrator! I smiled as I flew to Senegal, knowing that in a few days after returning, I would be doing the very job that I had wanted for twenty years.

I am confident that if I had not become a missionary for FamilyLife, I would never have become the church administrator at BCLR.

CHAPTER 27

Principle # 20 – Be Good Parents

Entire books are written on this topic, but I would like to highlight what Proverbs mentions.

We need to know our children (Proverbs 27:23).

"Know well"

- » To be concerned with; to have an intensive involvement with them. This exceeds a simple cognitive relationship with them.

"The condition"

- » The word "condition" literally means the appearance or face of a person; we look deeply in their faces, to know them well.

"Of your flocks, and pay attention to your herds."

- » Set your mind; to involve ourselves fully and personally with our herd (your children); this will take energy and discipline.

We need to train them in the light of Proverbs 22:6
Don't forget what I have said before, Proverbs contain principles that are generally true, but they are not promises to be claimed.

"Train up"

- » The Hebrew verb translated "train" occurs three other times in the Bible. In each of these, it refers to "dedicating" houses (Deuteronomy 20:5; 1 Kings 8:63; 2 Chronicles 7:5). When a house is dedicated, it is set aside for a certain purpose. When we dedicate or train up our children for the Lord, we are purposing to raise them up to be useful in God's Kingdom.

- » I also found in my studies that in non-biblical Hebrew literature, this term is also used to describe the action of a midwife who, soon after the child's birth, would dip her fingers into the juice of crushed dates and massage the infant's gums and palate. The tangy taste created a sensation of sucking. Then she would place the child in the mother's arms to begin nursing.

- » Likewise, parents are to create a thirst for God and your wisdom and counsel.

- » Every child's future is filled with possibilities. Parents have an opportunity to direct a child's path. Your response should be to pray and pray more. Watch and watch more. Discuss with your spouse the direction that we should take with respect to each child.

- » Remember, their temperaments are already built in by God. He is the one who created them. Not you! You must be sensitive to their characteristics (Psalm 139:13-16).

- » Diane and I spent lots of time in prayer concerning "the way" our children should go.

"A child"

- » The Hebrew term could mean anyone from newborn to marrying age.

"In the way"

- » In keeping with; in cooperation with; in accordance with something.

- » It is not just the path that they are on. It is also referring to the way God has created them.

- » "There are three things which are too wonderful for me, four which I do not understand: The way of an eagle in the sky, the way of a serpent on a rock, the way of a ship in the middle of the sea, and the way of a man with a maid" (Proverbs 30:18-19).

"He should go"

- » It is not your way, but the way created by God (Ephesians 2:10).

- » Just because the dad wanted a pro football player for a son, that should not mean he can ignore his son's gifting and abilities (i.e., talent for playing musical instruments, etc.).

- » This requires an enormous amount of patience, time, energy, concentration, and most importantly, prayer.

- » Remember: they are not a hunk of clay of which you can make anything you want; they are unique and fashioned by God! (Psalm 139:13-18).

PAPA MIKE'S PRAYER:

Lord, be with my children and grandchildren. Help each one as you present them with the challenge of parenting. May they be dedicated and sensitive to You. May You give them Your wisdom, understanding, patience, and endurance during their parenting years. Help them to remember that each decision has impact, and each nondecision is a decision. May their children respond to their efforts and follow You with a whole heart. Amen.

PAPA MIKE'S COMMENTS:

Most of you are not parents, so how can you apply this to yourself?

Parents sometimes make mistakes. Be patient and honor them.

Listen to them with an understanding ear. Think through what you are going to say. Be careful with your attitudes, actions, and emotions.

Don't clam up; that will not help at all.

Pray that God would help everyone communicate well.

CHAPTER 28

Principle #21 - What Causes and Eliminates Strife

What does God think about one who spreads strife?

> "A worthless person, a wicked man, is the one who walks with a perverse mouth, who winks with his eyes, who signals with his feet, who points with his fingers; who with perversity in his heart continually devises evil, who spreads strife. Therefore his calamity will come suddenly; instantly he will be broken and there will be no healing. There are six things which the Lord hates, yes, seven which are an abomination to Him: [1] Haughty eyes, [2] a lying tongue, [3] and hands that shed innocent blood, [4] a heart that devises wicked plans, [5] feet that run rapidly to evil, [6] a false witness who utters lies, [the following is an abomination to God] and one who spreads strife among brothers" (Proverbs 6:12-19). [Brackets are the author's.]

God delights in unity!

> "Behold, how good and how pleasant it is for brothers to dwell together in unity!" (Psalm 133:1).

What causes strife (discord)?

- » Arrogance (Proverbs 13:10a; 28:25a)

- » Anger (Proverbs 15:18a; 29:22a; 30:33)

- » Deceit and fraud (Proverbs 16:28a)
- » Hatred (Proverbs 10:12a)
- » Rebellion (Proverbs 17:19a)
- » Fool's lips (Proverbs 18:6a)
- » Contentiousness (Proverbs 26:21)

What eliminates strife?

- » "The beginning of strife is like letting out water, so abandon the quarrel before it breaks out. (Proverbs 17:14).
- » "The cast lot puts an end to strife and decides between the mighty ones. (Proverbs 18:18).
- » "Drive out a scoffer, and contention will go out, even strife and dishonor will cease." (Proverbs 22:10).

PAPA MIKE'S COMMENTS:

Thoughts on resolving conflicts. We will all have conflicts.

- » Have you ever felt misunderstood?
- » Have you ever been hurt by what another person said?
- » Have you ever felt like you haven't been heard?
- » Have you ever been betrayed?
- » Have you ever had to work through a misunderstanding?
- » Have you ever disagreed on a decision?
- » Have you ever held a grudge?
- » Have you ever been let down?

- » Have you ever felt like the other person doubted your commitment?
- » Have you ever felt used?

Some over-the-top comments concerning conflicts:

- » Conflicts with others are one of God's mysterious, counterintuitive ways of rescuing us from ourselves.
- » Conflicts can be used by God to defeat sin in us and make us more like Christ.
- » Conflicts can increase the closer we are with someone.
- » Conflicts can help us think through what we believe or think (Proverbs 18:15).
- » Conflicts can help us work harder at communicating effectively.
- » Conflicts can produce maturity and endurance (James 1:2-5).
- » Conflicts can sharpen one another (Proverbs 27:17).
- » Conflicts can strengthen our faith in the truth that God is working all things together for good (Romans 8:28).
- » Conflicts can give us the opportunity to practice servanthood (John 13:5-11) and preferring one another (Romans 12:10; Philippians 2:3-5).
- » Conflicts can give us the opportunity to love and glorify God (1 Corinthians 10:31).

What should be our goal in a conflict?

Unbiblical goals:

- » To get your way
- » To rationalize your actions
- » To prove yourself right
- » To prove another person wrong

- » To punish the other person
- » To pay back for a previous offense
- » To vent anger

Biblical goals:

- » To glorify God (1 Corinthians 10:13)
- » To please God (Psalm 9:5)
- » To become more like Christ (Romans 8:28-29; Colossians 1:28)
- » To build the other person up (study the life of Barnabas.)

What should our response not be once we are in a conflict?

- » We should not avoid the conflict or pretend that it does not exist. If we avoid or pretend that it does not exist, how is that going to solve anything?
- » Keeping quiet. Yes, sometimes we need to be quiet, but not often. Usually this only prolongs the conflict and makes it worse.
- » Staying away from the other person. If we do this long enough, we will not have a relationship.
- » Changing the subject or never talking about it. Avoidance does nothing to repair a relationship.
- » Waiting until the other person confesses their sins and then we (1) don't have to do anything, (2) can accept some responsibility, but not for everything, or (3) blame them for your sinful reaction.

What should our response be?

- » We should demonstrate love, care, and concern during times of disagreements (Romans 12:9-10; 1 Corinthians 13:4-8).
- » We should try to understand the other person's perspective. (See the section on understanding each other in Principle #12 on pages 150-151.)
- » We should pray, study, and think about the issue before speaking (Proverbs 15:1, 4, 23, 28; 18:21; 21:23; 25:11).

We should approach the other person correctly.

- » In matters of sin, approach the person in love (Ephesians 4:15), with gentleness and humility (Galatians 6:1–2. Make sure you have confessed any sin that might have contributed to the conflict.

- » In matters of preference, conviction, or conscience, prefer one another (Romans 12:10), and don't put a stumbling block in another person's way (Romans 14:13).
  From Diane's and my perspective, in a marriage, the one with the tightest conviction should be the one we follow until it has been discussed and agreed to by both parties that we want to change (Romans 14).

- » In matters of wisdom, I suggest searching the Scriptures (Acts 17:10–11; 2 Timothy 2:15), obtaining godly counsel (Proverbs 11:14; 12:15; 24:6), and praying to the Lord (Psalm 5:8; 25:5; 27:11; 143:10).

What should you remember?[4]

- » Tomorrow will only be better, if today we fix what was broken yesterday.

- » It is easier to rebuild a day or two of neglect than to rebuild years of neglect.

- » Will you commit to rebuild no matter how many years of neglect the relationship has experienced?

- » It is never too late to make a fresh beginning.

---

[4] Philip De Courcy, *Sermons on Nehemiah*. Kindred Community Church, https://www.kindredchurch.org/sermons/_scripture/nehemiah.

CHAPTER 29

Principle #22 – Be a Good Neighbor

- » Don't lie to your neighbor (3:28).
- » Don't devise harm to your neighbor (3:29).
- » Don't destroy your neighbor with your mouth (11:9).
- » Don't despise your neighbor (11:12; 14:21).
- » Be a guide to your neighbor (12:26).
- » Don't entice your neighbor (16:29).
- » Don't be a witness against your neighbor without cause (24:28).
- » Don't bear false witness against your neighbor (25:18).
- » Don't deceive your neighbor (26:19).
- » Don't flatter your neighbor (29:5).

PAPA MIKE'S ASSIGNMENT:

Who is your neighbor? Read the parable of the good Samaritan (Luke 10:25-37).

_____

_____

_____

_____

CHAPTER 30

Three Last Principles

Principle #23 – Be a Blessing to Your Parents

"A wise son makes a father glad, but a foolish son is a grief to his mother" (Proverbs 10:1).

"A wise son makes a father glad, but a foolish man despises his mother" (Proverbs 15:20).

"A foolish son is a grief to his father and bitterness to her who bore him" (Proverbs 17:25).

"A foolish son is destruction to his father" (Proverbs 19:13a).

"He who assaults his father and drives his mother away is a shameful and disgraceful son" (Proverbs 19:26).

"The father of the righteous will greatly rejoice, and he who sires a wise son will be glad in him" (Proverbs 23:24).

> "He who keeps the law is a discerning son, but he who is a companion of gluttons humiliates his father" (Proverbs 28:7).

Principle #24 – Be Joyful and Cheerful

> "A joyful heart makes a cheerful face, but when the heart is sad, the spirit is broken" (Proverbs 15:13).

> "All the days of the afflicted are bad, but a cheerful heart has a continual feast" (Proverbs 15:15).

> "A joyful heart is good medicine, but a broken spirit dries up the bones" (Proverbs 17:22).

Principle #25 – Leave an Inheritance

> "A good man leaves an inheritance to his children's children, and the wealth of the sinner is stored up for the righteous" (Proverbs 13:22).

> "House and wealth are an inheritance from fathers, but a prudent wife is from the Lord" (Proverbs 19:14).

- » Inheritance and a legacy go hand in hand.
- » Memorial stones can be part of a person's legacy.
- » This Bible study is a memorial stone for the people receiving it.

PART 3

CONCLUSION

Implementing this Bible study, which is a difficult thing to do because I have been working on it for over twelve years, two things come to mind that I would like to challenge you with:

- » We will all leave a legacy.

- » The importance of memorial stones.

LEGACY

- » Each of us will leave a legacy. It might be a good one or a poor one, but without a doubt, we will leave a legacy.

- » Our legacy may not be as widespread as that of a CEO of a major corporation or a pastor of a 5,000-member church, but for those it touches, it will be just as monumental.

- » For our legacy to impact others for Jesus Christ and His Kingdom, it will require thought, preparation, time, follow-through, and, most of all, a touch of God.

- » For most of us, our greatest potential legacy will be established through our children.

- » I encourage you to look back and remember people who had an impact on your life.

I certainly can:

- » Mrs. Maxie, my fourth-grade teacher at Forest Park Elementary School in Little Rock.

- » Mr. Berry, my advanced biology teacher at Hall High in Little Rock.

- » Pastor Bill Darnell in Houston – 1976 to 1979.

- » Pastor David Hocking in Los Angeles – 1979 to 1981.

- » And many others who all left their mark on this man.

My dad and mom left me a strong legacy that has stayed with me to this day.

Dad:

1. Be responsible.

    - » As I was growing up, my dad modeled this quality every day of his life. He never "played" much. That is not to say that he would not play with me or my sisters. But just for him to play by himself wasn't in his makeup. He was always doing something productive.

    > "Moreover, it is required of stewards that one be found trustworthy [or faithful]" (1 Corinthians 4:2). [Brackets are the author's.]

2. Be a hard worker.

    - » Yes, this is like the first, but one that I must highlight. I remember many times when I was growing up, being "taken" to work at one of my dad's friend's houses to help him dig, move, build, and we never had many breaks. I hope you did catch that little word "taken." There was no volunteer army at the Hefner household. And my dad did not care how small I was; he expected me to work and to work hard. Again, I thank him for instilling hard work into my life because it has served me well.

    > "Whatever you do, work heartily, as for the Lord rather than for men" (Colossians 3:23).

The next three are for both Dad and Mom:

3. Be friendly.

    - » Neither my dad nor my mom ever met a stranger. They would speak to anyone. On a trip to New Zealand, they met a couple and got to be friends. Later, that couple visited them in Sallisaw, Oklahoma. When my dad was eighty-one years old, he was known as the friendly old man who gave away mints.

> "A man that hath friends must shew himself friendly" (Proverbs 18:24 KJV).

4. Be hospitable.
   - » If anyone came to our house around mealtime, Mom would always invite them to sit down and eat, even when there was not much food on the table. She would make it work. On Saturday morning, Dad's friends would always come to the back door, knock, push the door open, and call out for Dad. Dad welcomed them and offered them a cup of coffee and some breakfast.

   > "Contributing to the needs of the saints, practicing hospitality (Romans 12:13).

   > "Do not neglect to show hospitality to strangers, for by this some have entertained angels without knowing it" (Hebrews 13:2).

5. Be generous.
   - » Mom and Dad were both generous, but for much of our growing-up years, we did not have much money. Therefore, their giving came through ways other than money. Mostly it was with their time. They were always willing to help.
   - » For my dad: I do not remember the circumstances, but I do remember one day in our kitchen that my dad really did give the shirt off his back to one of his friends.
   - » For my mom: I remember one time walking into her bedroom, and I noticed that she only had three or four dresses in her closet, while I knew my sisters had lots of dresses.
   - » Once again, God used these examples to forge a spirit of generosity in this man's heart.

   > "He who is generous will be blessed" (Proverbs 22:9a).

The next two are for Mom:

6. Be a servant to family and others.

    » She never stopped serving. I remember her sewing late into the night to finish my sister's dresses for some big event. My dad was a diabetic for fifty-eight years, so that is when mom started cooking three full meals a day. I bet in my mom's lifetime, she cooked my dad over 50,000 home-cooked meals, and I never heard her once complain. No, not once. What a servant. What an attitude! What a legacy!

    » Jesus washed his disciples' feet (John 13:4-12 ESV).

7. Be loving and caring.

    I would like to let you see how she showed love and care to this man as a boy.

    » The only sport I ever played was Little League baseball, and I remember my mom sitting in the stands every game, even in the hot days of August in Little Rock, Arkansas, and never once did I hear her complain. She always stayed and cheered, even though there was not much to cheer about since I was such a little guy.

    » I remember coming home from elementary school, and she would often meet me, and we would talk about my day. She would give me a Coke and some cookies and just listen to this little boy.

    » And finally, I must tell you about her patience and love with me and my spelling. You see, I have dyslexia, and when I was growing up, very little was known about the condition. I remember my mom spending hours with me each week going over my twenty spelling words, and I would still miss between five to eight words. But I can't remember a time where she got frustrated or called me any name. She just loved me! She truly modeled Christ's love to this son, and to that end, I will be eternally grateful.

I would like to encourage you to think through what qualities you would like your children to attribute to you someday in the future.

MEMORIAL STONES

God has been using memorial stones ever since the beginning of time.

God initiated:

- » Memorialization of His covenant between us and Him – the rainbow after the flood (Genesis 9).

- » Memorialization of His rules and ways – the tablets that "the Law" was written on (Exodus 20).

- » Memorialization of man's new birth in Christ – Christian baptism (Romans 6).

- » Memorialization of the Lord's death, burial, and resurrection – the Lord's Supper
(1 Corinthians 11).

- » Memorialization of great events where God has shown Himself strong – the twelve stones (Joshua 4).

> Take for yourselves twelve men from the people, one man from each tribe, and command them, saying, 'Take up for yourselves twelve stones from here out of the middle of the Jordan, from the place where the priests' feet are standing firm, and carry them over with you and lay them down in the lodging place where you will lodge tonight.' Let this be a sign among you, so that when your children ask later, saying, 'What do these stones mean to you?' then you shall say to them,

> 'Because the waters of the Jordan were cut off before the ark of the covenant of the Lord; when it crossed the Jordan, the waters of the Jordan were cut off.' So these stones shall become a memorial to the sons of Israel forever.
> (Joshua 4:2-3, 6-7)

Memorial stones were used by God to help us remember what He has done for us.

A verse that also had a tremendous impact on me was Hebrews 11:4:

> "By faith Abel offered to God a better sacrifice than Cain, through which he obtained the testimony that he was righteous, God testifying about his gifts, and through faith, though he is dead, he still speaks."

I see memorial stones as a tangible way for me to be an encouragement to my children and friends long after I have gone to be with Jesus.

The first memorial stone I gave to my children was a family crest that I created. Katherine White painted the one for Aaron, and Katherine Spena painted the one for Marcie, Ben, Diane, and I. Both women were very good friends of the family, and they still are. I gave Aaron and Lindsay and Ben and Jody their family crests during the rehearsal dinner for their weddings. I gave Blair and Marcie theirs a few days before their wedding. I got the idea from Robert Lewis's book, *Raising a Modern Day Knight: A Father's Role in Guiding His Son to Authentic Manhood*.[5]

The Hefner Crest

Please see the back cover for a picture of the one that Katherine Spena painted.

- » Above the shield – victor's crown (1 Corinthians 15:57).

- » Top of the shield – ribbon with letters (1 Peter 2:21).

- » Bottom of the shield – ribbon with letters (1 Corinthians 10:31).

- » Inside the shield: hands praying (constantly praying), staff (leading like a shepherd), open Bible (studying with a passion), towel and water (serving with humility)

I have given them other memorials.

---
5   Robert Lewis. *Raising a Modern-Day Knight*. Focus on the Family, 1996.

When Ben and Jody left Little Rock for Chicago without a job to help two friends start a church, I gave them a statue that depicted Peter leaving his boat to follow Christ. Ben is now one of the full-time pastors at that church.

To see one of these statues, click the link below:

- https://scottstearman.com/wp-content/uploads/2020/04/calling_front1.jpg

All three of my kids went through a tough time between 2014 and 2015. This was also a very hard time for us as their parents because in each case, we couldn't do anything except pray. And we did pray!

Aaron and Lindsay:
Had to leave Senegal, West Africa, where they had faithfully served for ten years. Aaron started his training is 1998, and they came home in April 2015.

Blair and Marcie:
Had one of their twins pass away at childbirth in February 2015.

Ben and Jody:
Went to Chicago to help a couple of friends start a church. They left in June 2014, but Ben could not find a job in his field for ten months. During that time, he worked at Target, made furniture, and did all kinds of other odd jobs to make ends meet.

In July of 2015, we had a family reunion at Marcie's home in Colorado. During the family reunion, each couple shared their story. At the end of the time, I gave each couple a crystal clock with the following things engraved on them:

On Aaron's and Lindsay's:
- Enduring Steadfastness – Psalm 62:1-2, 5-8
  Aaron and Lindsay
  2014-2015

On Blair's and Marcie's:
- Trust God in Troubles – Job 1:20-22; 2:10; 42:1-3
  Blair and Marcie
  2015

On Ben's and Jody's:
- Trust and Obedience – Psalm 37:3-6
  Ben and Jody
  2014-2015

If you want to see what one of these clocks looks like, click the link below:

I have given other memorial stones to Diane, my children, and lots of my friends. Each one has been a joy for me to give.

Besides the family crest, the two that are most memorable are the ones I have given to Diane. One was associated with our twenty-fifth wedding anniversary, and the other was on her sixty-fifth birthday.

Our twenty-fifth anniversary was on June 11, 2002.

In February 2002, I started thinking about what I could do to honor this woman who had given so much to me! I first wrote down all the ways in which I was so grateful for her. It was not hard at all. When I finished, I had it framed as a gift to her on our special day. Today, it is hanging in our den.

I then decided I wanted to have a party where I could share my thoughts with her and our closest friends.

In thinking, planning, and writing, the theme of the evening came to me: TIME.

I started thinking about a special gift. In February, a local jewelry store put on sale an hourglass necklace with little diamond chips as the sand. It was beautiful, and it was perfect for my theme. It was a God thing! The gift was going to be a "memorial stone" for our twenty-fifth anniversary and symbolized the following things with respect to my theme of "TIME":

» First, the time we have spent together.

» Second, a reminder that we need to redeem the time. (Ephesians 5:16).

» Third, an admonition to count our days and realize that time and eternity are just around the corner (Psalm 90:12).

- » Fourth, we want to build our lives on precious stones, such as gold and diamonds, and not on wood, hay, and stubble (1 Corinthians 3:12-13).

- » Fifth, and finally, my life would not have been complete or useful without you, just like this hourglass would not have been complete or useful without the diamonds inside (Ecclesiastes 3:12).

The Kipps hosted my dinner party. I invited forty people and had Aaron and Marcie fly home. Diane knew I was planning something but did not know all the details. It was a great evening!

Now, I come to the second memorial stone.

I wanted to give Diane something very special on her sixty-fifth birthday, something that would tell her how I feel about her and what she means to me. I worked with Michael Fuqua, a dear friend, to design and create a one-of-a-kind piece of jewelry.

Since we had gone to Israel a couple of years before, I wanted the gift to be a reminder of our trip. I decided on a necklace with a coin that, if possible, was minted during the time of Christ.

Michael had a bag of old coins, and one morning, I looked through the bag and found a beautiful silver coin. He researched it and found that it was a denarius, and it was minted between 20 BC and 20 AD. A true God thing! I told him I also wanted a diamond to be part of the necklace. He came up with the idea of using a 65-point diamond. One point for each year of her life. I loved the idea! Another blessing of the Lord came when Michael had a 65-point diamond in his inventory. Then he got to work, and the creation was born. It was prettier than I could have ever imagined. It was perfect. I then wrote how this piece of jewelry symbolized what Diane meant to me.

The necklace itself:

You are one of God's most beautiful creations, and I could not have asked for a more perfect gift (Psalm 139:13-18), friend (Proverbs 17:17) and wife (Proverbs 31:10–31). What a blessing you have been to me for our forty-five years of marriage.

The beautiful gold chain:

- » The gold does not compare to the wisdom that you have given to me ever since I met you in 1974 (Proverbs 16:16).

The 65-point exquisite diamond:

- » Each point represents one of the years of your life.

- » The diamond does not compare to your worth to me (Proverbs 31:10).

The silver coin was produced sometime between 20 BC and 20 AD by the Roman Emperor Caesar Augustus. The coin represents:

- » When Jesus Christ was born (Luke 2:1-7).

- » The purpose for Him coming to earth (Acts 2:22-24).

- » Your initial condition (Romans 3:10-18).

- » You accepted His free gift of salvation in 1972 (Ephesians 2:8-9).

Thank you, Diane, for being my wife, friend, lover, partner in ministry, and sister in Christ. I look forward to each day God gives us on this earth, knowing that one day we will both be in heaven praising our Lord together forever.

Thank you, Diane, for being my wife.

Mike

BOOKS THAT HAVE IMPACTED MY LIFE

Two authors of the '80s had a significant impact on my spiritual growth:

John MacArthur

- » I listened to *Grace to You* and purchased every one of his study guides during the '80s.

- » MacArthur, John. *The Gospel According to Jesus: What Is Authentic Faith?*. Academic Books, 1988.

- » I have all his commentaries, and they have been a real blessing to me.

Charles Swindoll

- » I listened to *Insight for Living* and purchased all of his study guides.

- » *Improving Your Serve: The Art of Unselfish Living.* Word Books, 1981.

- » *Dropping Your Guard: The Value of Open Relationships.* Word Books, 1983.

- » *Hand Me Another Brick: Timeless Lessons on Leadership.* Word Books, 1983.

» *Living on the Ragged Edge: Finding Joy in a World Gone Mad.* Word Books, 1985.

» *Living Above the Level of Mediocrity: A Commitment to Excellence.* Word Books, 1987.

I love his books on the characters of the Bible. I have all of them.

One other person who had a significant impact on my spiritual growth was David Hocking.

» I went to his church from April 1979 through April 1981. At that time, my company moved me to West Virginia, and the teaching was not near as good as David's. I knew David, so I called and told him my situation. For the next four years he had his staff send me all his messages. What a blessing!

During that time, I was also impacted by the following books:

» Andelin, Audrey. *A Man of Steel and Velvet.* Pacific Press, 1972.

» Gire, Ken. *Moments with the Savior.* Zondervan Press, 1998.

» Morgan, G. Campbell. *The Great Physician.* Flemming H. Revell Company, 1982.

» Piper, John. *Desiring God.* Multnomah Press, 1986.

1990s:

» Lewis, Robert. *Raising a Modern-Day Knight.* Focus on the Family, 1996.

» Maxwell, John. *Developing the Leader Within You.* Thomas Nelson, 1993.

» Maxwell, John. *Developing the Leaders Around You.* Thomas Nelson, 1995.

» Piper, John. *A Godward Life.* Multnomah Books, 1997.

» Piper, John. *A Godward Life Book Two.* Multnomah Books, 1999.

» Swindoll, Charles. *Man to Man.* Zondervan Press, 1997.

» Weber, Stu. *Tender Warrior.* Multnomah Books, 1993.

Early 2000s

- » Alcorn, Randy. *Heaven.* Tyndale House Publishers, Inc., 2004.
- » Alcorn, Randy. *Money, Possessions, and Eternity.* Tyndale House Publishers, Inc., 1989.
- » MacArthur, John. *Faith Works: The Gospel According to the Apostles.* W Publishing Group, 1993.
- » MacArthur, John. *The Murder of Jesus.* W Publishing Group, 2000.
- » MacArthur, John. *Twelve Ordinary Men.* W Publishing Group, 2002.
- » MacArthur, John. *The Book on Leadership.* Thomas Nelson, Inc., 2004.
- » MacArthur, John. *Slave: The Hidden Truth About Your Identity in Christ.* Thomas Nelson, 2010.
- » Piper, John. *What Jesus Demands from the World.* Crossway Books, 2006.
- » Scott, Stuart. *The Exemplary Husband – Revised Edition.* Focus Publishing, Inc., 2002.

In 2002, I got involved in biblical counseling. I attended conferences and got the full Christian Counseling Commentaries set by Jay Adams.

- » Faith Baptist Church, Lafayette, IN. Teaching from Biblical Counseling Conferences: Steve Viars, Brent Aucoin, Brad Bigney, Paul David Tripp, Lou Priolo.
- » Adams, Jay. *The Christian Counseling Commentaries - 10 volumes.* Institute for Nouthetic Studies, 1999.

Here are a few of the biblical counseling books that I have read:

- » Arterburn, Stephen and Fred Stoeker. *Every Man's Battle.* WaterBroker Press, 2000.
- » Bigney, Brad. Gospel *Treason: Betraying the Gospel with Hidden Idols.* P and R Publishing, 2012.

- Bridges, Charles. *Proverbs. Banner of Truth Trust*, 1846.

- Bridges, Jerry. *Trusting God*. NavPress, 1998.

- Carder, Dave. *Torn Asunder*. Moody Publishers, 2008.

- Challies, Tim. *Sexual Detox: A Guide for Guys Who Are Sick of Porn*. Cruciform Press, 2010.

- DeMoss, Nancy Leigh. *Choosing Gratitude*. Moody Publishers, 2009.

- DeMoss, Nancy Leigh. *Choosing Forgiveness*. Moody Publishers, 2006.

- DeYoung, Kevin. *Taking God at His Word*. Crosswa,y 2014.

- Fitzpatrick, Elyse. *Idols of the Heart*. P & R Publishing, 2001.

- Harris, Joshua. *Not Even a Hint*. Multnomah Publishers, 2003.

- Jones, Robert. *Uprooting Anger*. P & R Publishing, 2005.

- Lane, Tim and Paul David Tripp. *How People Change*. New Growth Press, 2008.

- Lane, Tim and Paul David Tripp. *Relationships: A Mess Worth Making*. New Growth Press, 2006.

- Lambert, Heath. *Finally Free: Fighting for Purity with the Power of Grace*. Zondervan, 2013.

- MacDonald, James. *I Really Want to Change*. Moody Press, 2000.

- Mack, Wayne A. *Humility: The Forgotten Virtue*. P & R Publishing, 2005.

- Mack, Wayne A. *Anger and Stress Management God's Way*. Calvary Press, 2004.

- Mack, Wayne A. *Homework Manual for Biblical Living, Volume 1*. P & R Publishing, 1979.

- Mack, Wayne A. *Homework Manual for Biblical Living, Volume 2*. P & R Publishing, 1980.

- Mahaney, C.J. *Humility: True Greatness*. Multnomah Publishers, 2005.
- Ortund, Raymond C., Jr. *Proverbs: Wisdom that Works*. Crossway, 2012.
- Piper, John. *This Momentary Marriage*. Crossway Books, 2009.
- Powlison, David. *Seeing with New Eyes*. P & R Publishing, 2003.
- Powlison, David. *Speaking Truth in Love*. Punch Press, 2005.
- Priolo, Lou. *Helping Keep Your Cool*. P & R Publishing, 2006.
- Sande, Ken. *Peace Maker*. Baker Books, 1991.
- Shaw, Mark. *Addiction-Proof Parenting*. Focus Publishing, 2010.
- Shaw, Mark. *The Heart of Addiction – A Biblical Perspective*. Focus Publishing, 2008.
- Selvaggio, Anthony. *A Proverbs Driven Life*. Shepherd Press, 2008.
- Stoop, David. *Forgiving The Unforgivable*. Servant Publications, 2003.
- Tripp, Paul David. *A Quest for More*. New Growth Press, 2007.
- Tripp, Paul David. *War of Words*. P & R Publishing, 2000.
- Tripp, Paul David. *Instruments in the Redeemer's Hands*. P & R Publishing, 2002.
- Viars, Stephen. *Putting your Past in Its Place*. Harvest House Publishers, 2011.
- Welch, Edward T. *Blame It on the Brain*. P & R Publishing, 1998.
- Welch, Edward T. *Depression A Stubborn Darkness*. New Growth Press, 2004.
- Welch, Edward T. *Side by Side*. Crossway, 2015.
- Welch, Edward T. *When People are Big and God Is Small*. P & R Publishing, 1997.
- Welch, Edward T. *Addictions A Banquet in the Grave*. P & R Publishing, 2001.

- » Whitney, Donald. *Spiritual Disciplines of the Christian Life*. NavPress, 1991.
- » Yawn, Byron Forrest. *What Every Man Wishes His Father Had Told Him*. Harvest House Publishing, 2012.

Here are some of the books I read on parenting during 2012 and 2016:

- » Bruner, Olivia and Kurt. *Playstation Nation*. Center Street, 2006.
- » Chapman, Gary and Arlene Pellicane. *Growing Up Social*. Northfield Publishing, 2014.
- » Crouch, Andy. *Tech Wise Family*. Baker Books, 2017.
- » Dean, Paul and Alan Melton. *Disciple Like Jesus for Parents*. Calvary Press, 2009.
- » Elmore, Tim. *12 Huge Mistakes Parents Can Avoid: Leading Your Kids to Succeed in Life*. Harvest House Publishers, 2014.
- » Elmore, Tim. *Generation iY: Secrets to Connecting with Today's Teens & Young Adults in the Digital Age Expanded Edition*. Poet Gardener Publishing, 2015.
- » Elmore, Tim. *Artificial Maturity: Helping Kids Meet the Challenge of Becoming Authentic Adults*. Jossey-Bass, 2012.
- » Farley, William P. *Gospel-Powered Parenting*. P & R Publishing, 2009.
- » Harvey, Dave. *When Sinners Say "I Do."* Shepherd Press, 2007.
- » Hughes, Kent and Barbara. *Disciplines of a Godly Family*. Crossway, 2007.
- » Kimmel, Tim. *Why Christian Kids Rebel*. W Publishing Group, 2004.
- » Kimmel, Tim. *Raising Kids for True Greatness*. W Publishing Group, 2006.
- » MacArthur, John. *Successful Christian Parenting*. Word Publishing, 1998.
- » Plowman, Ginger. *Don't Make Me Count to Three*. Shepherd Press, 2003.
- » Priolo, Lou. *Getting a Grip*. Calvary Press Publishing, 2006.

- Priolo, Lou. *Teach Them Diligently*. Timeless Text, 2006.

- Priolo, Lou. *The Heart of Anger*. Calvary Press Publishing, 1997.

- Reinke, Tony. *12 Ways Your Phone Is Changing You*. Crossway, 2017.

- Rosemond, John. *Parenting by the Book*. Howard Books, 2007.

- Scott, Stuart. *The Exemplary Husband Revised Addition*. Focus Publishing, 2002.

- Scott, Stuart and Martha Peace. *The Faithful Parent: A Biblical Guide to Raising a Family*. P & R Publishing, 2010.

- Tripp, Paul David. *Age of Opportunity*. P & R Publishing, 1997.

- Tripp, Paul David. *Parenting: 14 Gospel Principles*. Crossway, 2016.

- Tripp, Paul David. *Getting to the Heart of Parenting* (DVDs). Paul David Tripp Ministries 2009.

- Tripp, Tedd and Margy. *Instructing a Child's Heart*. Shepherd Press, 2008.

- Tripp, Tedd. *Shepherding a Child's Heart*. Shepherd Press, 1995.

- Thomas, Gary L. *Sacred Parenting*. Zondervan, 2004.

- Turansky, Scott and Joanne Miller. *Say Goodbye to Whining, Complaining, and Bad Attitudes in You and Your Kids*. Water Brook Press, 2000.

- Weber, Stu. *The Warrior Soul*. Charisma House, 2015.

- Welch, Kristen. *Raising Grateful Kids in an Entitled World*. Tyndale Momentum, 2015.